SPIRITUAL LIFE RAFTS

Women's Stories of Profound Loss, Courage and Healing

by JUDY WOLF

Interfaith Minister

This book is dedicated to my family, Rob, Joe and Tommy, without whom, I would have only the faintest notion of what it means to love, and to be loved, in this lifetime.

In Gratitude

Thank you Bobbi Dumas for your masterful reshaping of these stories and insightful editing; Thank you Susan O'Shaugnessy for your fine writing contribution and your encouragement from start to finish; Thank you Sharon, Lonnie, Carol and friends for sustaining me through our long hospital stay; Thank you Greg for moving mountains; Thank you Michelle and my prayer circle for nudging me to write this book.

Cover design and illustration by Jehiah Bray
Printing by Book Printers of Utah
Typesetting and design by Design Type Service

ISBN 978-0-9801735-0-5

INSTITUTE

Proceeds from the sale of *Spiritual Life Rafts* will be donated to The Institute for Spirituality and Healing in Medicine (SHIM) to further their mission. To order additional copies of this book, or for group discounts, visit *www.theshim institute.org,* email *wendyfanderson@hotmail.com,* or phone 801.268.1068.

Who Are We? The SHIM Institute promotes the connection of mind, body and spirit for the purpose of creating a supportive healing environment, tailored to the needs of the patient, thus reinforcing their resiliency and vitality for life. We define SPIRITUALITY as the dimension of a person that seeks to find internal meaning and purpose in their life, through their relationships . . . with themselves, with others, and with a Higher Power of their own understanding. The 7 SHIM Principles of Healing are Faith, Hope, Social Connectedness, Purpose, Control, Forgiveness and Gratitude. We believe in reinforcing the ideal of compassionate care in the patient/healthcare professional relationship.

We are interdisciplinary colleagues of different faiths educating healthcare professionals, patients and members of the care team, including family and friends, about the critical role spirituality plays in promoting optimum health and recovery. SHIM offers lectures, workshops and conferences and provides pertinent research and publications, through its website www.theshiminstitute.org.

Why Read Spiritual Life Rafts?

Advance praise for this book . . .

After 35 years of cancer patient care, I believe the principles in this book can literally mean the difference between life and death for a struggling patient and may bring unique comfort to their loved ones. A patchwork quilt of stories, the book beautifully demonstrates that we all heal differently, but share strikingly similar characteristics in our process. Pieced together, they share one powerful theme—resiliency in the face of great adversity, be it illness, injury, disease or death, relies in large part on one's active spirituality and desire to heal. This uplifting collection of the accounts of 14 women of a variety of faiths and traditions offers a helpful pathway to those dealing with loss or crisis, and those who want to help them—emotionally, spiritually, or both.

Jerry W. Sonkens, M.D.,
Fellow American College of Surgeons,
Head and Neck Cancer Surgeon, Founder SHIM

This book truly is a life raft, something to hang on to in the midst of one's own storm, or to throw to someone caught in the waves of suffering. What a comforting, affirming gift to know you are not alone in your suffering, and that others have healed from such heart-wrenching journeys. Long after my husband was seriously injured, I found each page to be an inspiring moment of grace. At some point in our lives, we, or someone we love, will need this book to keep us afloat through tumultuous, uncertain times.

Lori Giovannoni-Roper,
Author of Success Redefined, and The Law of Achievement
(with Kathleen Gage), Nationally Recognized Speaker,
Training and Development Consultant

One of the best things to have on the journey of life is a book about getting through our greatest difficulties using spiritual tools. These stories show how adversity can really be an opportunity for growth and spiritual empowerment, even though, at first glance, they appear to be heartbreaking stories of excruciating loss. The stories here are a lot like the experiences many of my patients have shared with me over my 25-year nursing career. Through others' struggles, we can discover more of ourselves and life itself. Inspiration can move us to look beyond the obvious and see the spiritual nature of all that is. From there we can live more fully, with hope and strength rekindled. This book is a beautiful light that shines brightly in the darkest of times.

Cathy Seegers, M.S., APRN,
Psychiatric/Mental Health and Family Nurse Practitioner

Attention all humans! Life is full of suffering . . . there is no question if you will suffer, but only when, how much, how long, and under what circumstances? There is no more affective teacher of the value of life than the loss of a loved one. I learned this most acutely when my brother, whom I adored, was killed by a new teenage driver while standing in his front yard. There is no more effective teacher of how people struggle with dignity after the loss of a loved one. Only humans are given the invitation to consider a bigger, eternal perspective, to be resilient, to recover and teach what they have learned to others. Judy Wolf combines affective and effective lessons of learning to cope, and continues to explore an ever-expanding perspective after the tragic, inexplicable loss of her child. The personal stories in this book will assist those who suffer a profound loss and are searching for a way to re-engage life more fully. The combined stories in the book speak to the human soul and comfort the brokenhearted.

Albert Zylstra, Ph.D. Psychology,
32 years as a School Psychologist, Principal of a middle school and a school for handicapped children.

In this book, we discover a variety of spiritual life rafts, to cling to and to lead us to healing, even in the midst of a perilous personal storm. Each story opens up a new insight, a new lesson, a new opportunity for learning and reflection. I applaud Judy for her courage and determination to explore the diverse, unique and sometimes unconventional spiritual tools that survivors use to heal themselves. I applaud everyone who takes the challenge to read this insightful, deeply personal book and discovers for themselves their own spiritual life rafts.

Jody Davis,
Hospice Chaplain

The strengths and experiences of the women in this book far exceed anything I, as a mother of five children, have experienced. Their resiliency, coping skills and strength are inspiring. They all have a unique way of surviving, sometimes relying on conventional faith and sometimes "borrowing and blending" spiritual practices from the world's wisdom traditions. There are no two who followed the same path to healing, but they all got there, in their own time, in their own way. These women are quiet heroes in the lives of their families and friends. Though I've never endured anything nearly so difficult or painful, I found some valuable lessons for my own life.

Wendy Anderson,
Executive Director, The SHIM Institute

Every experience in life offers an opportunity to discover something important about the purpose and meaning of life . . . the more difficult the experience, the richer the opportunity. These stories elucidate some of the toughest "life lessons" and plumb the depths of personal resilience and maturity of the soul. Read these stories with an open mind and heart—they contain an important message for you and those you want to help.

N. Lee Smith, M.D.,
Director, Stress Medicine and Lifetree Pain Clinic

Contents

Why I Wrote this Book

Miracle Healing. What does this mean to you? You probably have specific ideas. Christ laying his hands on a leper or raising Lazarus back to life. Or perhaps the modern miracle story of a man waking up from a coma 6 years after an accident.

And yet, I am amazed and touched by the simple miracle *of* healing, and the thousands of ways and paths that people choose to create that miracle when all seems lost.

Sometimes, some days, simply holding on is the miracle. Finding one thing that will keep you afloat, no matter how battered you are by the waves, no matter how easy you think it might be to slip under the water, into oblivion. I know. I've been there. It's hard and it hurts and you're certain no one knows what you're going through.

But I do. I may not know you, or the particular details of *your* story, but I understand.

Why did I write this book? I wrote it to honor myself, to heal myself. To honor my sons and my husband and our journey. To honor all people who have endured more than any person should be asked to.

Until seven years ago, I lived a charmed life, without even realizing it. I had a loving marriage, two beautiful, healthy boys, a strong, supportive circle of friends and a rewarding career.

We knew health and abundance. We thought that we knew God, and understood how He worked in our lives. We felt blessed. We weren't extravagant, but lived well. We had everything we could ask for.

Until the day my older son, Joe, was hit by a car. He was critically injured. We spent 16 months in hospitals trying to rehabilitate his severely damaged brain. Finally, we brought him home in a vegetative state, where we cared for him 24/7 for two more years until he died. (To read more about this story, see "Judy.")

I was ordained an Interfaith Minister two months after Joe died. As part of my seminary studies, which I'd undertaken as part of my own healing journey, I had been assigned the task of adopting different religions for a month at a time. Less concerned with what these religions "believed," we were asked to *experience* them. What spiritual practices did they offer, and how did these practices or rituals help us be more present to our own spirituality, our own experience of God (the God or Source of our own understanding)?

It was a perfect quest for me and would ultimately lead me to the very heart of my own spiritual questions. Where is the intersection of our religious beliefs, the boundaries of our theology, with how we choose to practice our beliefs, the daily steps we take in order to find comfort and help us heal? I know what you believe; now tell me what you do to breathe life into it? And how is that working for you in your everyday life?

In a way, it's the difference between *saying* a prayer, and *praying* a prayer, less in the words than in the connection to Spirit that inspires us to carry on, no matter what. This, to me, is where one's *spirituality* emerges, the point where one's soul connects intimately to the practice, rather than going through the motions because we're supposed to.

After Joe died, I needed to heal. But I also needed to find a new place to put my energy, my nurturing instincts, my time—all of the things that had been devoted to caring for him.

So as part of my own healing and the next step of my spiritual journey, I would seek out other women, women who had lost everything, or so it seemed. I would learn from them, how their religion and spirituality kept them afloat. What tools, practices and steps did they take to heal, regardless of their beliefs? Did they turn toward or away from their religion of origin? What role did human connection and community play, and what did they offer in the way of spiritual comfort?

Fueled by intellectual and spiritual curiosity, as well as the intense need to seek my own answers and, yes, even to keep myself busy, I set out to answer the question, *What works best?*

I sought women who had endured intense loss. I sought women of traditional faith, and women who spiritually bushwhacked their own paths. Formal theology or doctrine was only mildly interesting to me. I was looking for the place where religion intersected one's personal spiritual connection, no matter the belief system.

I sat with these women for hours. I asked questions, listened, and took notes; I cried and absorbed their painful lessons. I remain touched and blessed by them. I thank them from the depths of my soul for their generosity in sharing these messages of hope and perseverance, for helping me heal my shattered heart. And for allowing me to share their wisdom and grace in this book, in the hope it may help others.

I learned so much from them, these lovely, courageous women.

I learned that healing happens eventually, if you work at it.

I learned that while we will never be the same, we can be healthy, whole and joyful again.

Perhaps even before I began, I knew the truth about what works in promoting healing, but these women helped me understand it at depth:

What works best, is what works for you.

I also wrote this for my husband and son Tommy. I would like to add here that I could not have healed without them. Authors sometimes refer to their books as their babies, and I understand this now. This book is a labor of love that has taken three years to be born. Unlike a real child, though, once a book is born, it exists on its own, interacting with the world in its changeless form.

Children take much more long-term love and care. After Joe died, I transferred my intense nurturing instincts to Tommy, who, as a 14-year-old male, wanted nothing to do with them. (Surprise, surprise.) Tommy did not humor me, forcing me to redirect my restlessness. As he wryly told me, "Mom, you need to get a life!"

Tommy's road has also been one of great loss. Though I don't often discuss it with him, I admire his quiet strength and resilience; I am amazed by his maturity and grace. My husband and I lost a son, and we have another; Tommy lost his brother, and he has no other. He lost his best friend, roommate, partner-in-crime (though Joe was the real culprit), and the person I expected would be there for him for the rest of his life, in the way that brothers are. I am charmed by the person Tommy is turning out to be (maybe someday he'll even appreciate my saying that), and I sincerely hope he feels the loving presence of his big brother all the days of his life. He deserves it.

For all of the people who were there for us, who truly helped us heal, and were part of the miraculous journey I've come to know as Joe's life, I thank you. Sharon, especially you. These include so many people, from those who sent us prayers and hope via e-mail, and every person who read, sang to, or spent the night with Joe. It includes the people we knew about, and the ones who served quietly, anonymously from the sidelines. To our respective families, LDS and Unity church communities, our neighborhood, Waterford, Jordan Valley School, Primary Children's Medical Center, HealthSouth, our caregivers and pray-ers of all faiths, and none, thank you for holding us afloat through our darkest of storms.

And for those of you on the road to healing, who aren't quite sure you'll ever feel healthy, or whole or joyful again, I offer you the simple gift of this book. I hope and pray it will serve you in the way you need it, as a safe harbor in the storm you're weathering this moment, this day, for however long you may need it. And when you too reach the promised land, I'd ask that you turn and take the hand of the woman who walks behind you, the newcomer to the village well of loss, and pass on what you have learned about hope, courage, perseverance and healing.

"I believe there is an important distinction to be made between religion and spirituality. Religion I take to be concerned with belief in the claims to salvation of one faith tradition or another—an aspect of which is acceptance of some form of metaphysical or philosophical reality, including perhaps an idea of heaven or hell. Connected with this are religious teachings or dogma, ritual, prayers and so on. Spirituality I take to be concerned with those qualities of the human spirit—such as love and compassion, patience, tolerance, forgiveness, contentment, a sense of responsibility, a sense of harmony, which bring happiness to both self and others."

– His Holiness the Dalai Lama

CHAPTER ONE

Sally

For many, religion is a concept, a shared story among a congregation of believers, something that provides a spiritual road map for our human path. But when a storm hits, faith itself can become powerful, tangible and affirming. To the drowning, it can become a vital lifeline, the very thing that keeps them alive and engaged. And perhaps for the wisest and most spiritual among us, like Sally, faith becomes the very gift hidden in the clouds, the fabled silver lining:

I was raised Episcopalian, a spiritual, religious community that I've been a member of ever since. As a child, I went to Sunday school, worship service, and vacation bible school. My parents were active volunteers in the church and in various social welfare programs. My mother was very "out" about her Christianity, very vocal and upfront about what it meant to her and how she lived her faith through her actions. At the time I hardly noticed, but I understand now this was a powerful reflection of 'wearing one's faith' openly through kind words and acts of service, rather than dogma or proclamation.

Through my adult life, I've had many friends in 'search

mode', looking for a source of spiritual direction from a wide variety of sources, including crystals, tarot cards, astrology and the like. I have read and learned about other faiths, and I honor other beliefs, but I have never felt the need to question my own faith. It has worked for me, especially when I needed it most.

I married young, soon after high school, and moved with my husband to a new town. I was nineteen and everything felt strange and new, so I immediately sought comfort and connection in the local Episcopal Church. To me, church is a safe place to grow your extended family, to socialize, and to seek and offer comfort. I knew this truth instinctively, but it became clearer through the years, as I came to rely on the church's presence in my life.

Though my husband and I shared a common faith, we were very young and our marriage didn't survive. We divorced after a few years. I suffered through periodic bouts of depression, sleeplessness, fatigue and loss of appetite. As a young divorcee, I assumed my physical problems were due to stress and emotional turmoil, and my doctor agreed.

I turned to prayer, developing a comforting nightly ritual. I would ask God to help me relax, to help me sleep deeply and to take away my fear. Then I would feel the Spirit's presence, as if I was being wrapped in a fluffy cloud of protection. I'd never felt such peace, such security. I fell asleep easily. To this day, when I have trouble sleeping, I pray for His presence. He comes; I sleep.

Soon after my divorce, I moved to Redding, California to take a job with a company I'm still with today, 28 years later. Once again, I attended the local Episcopal Church, to worship, to meet people and to create an extended family. It worked. I felt so at home in this new community and even more connected to my faith and spirituality, an important element for me at the time, since I was thirty-five years old, divorced and living in a small town.

At the time, I maintained my nightly prayer ritual, concluding it with the request, "Lord, please send someone to love me and someone to love." It didn't seem very realistic, but if anyone could make it happen, I figured it was God. One Sunday morning in church, God spoke directly to me, plain as day: 'You will be loved.' I looked around to see if anyone else heard it; it was so real to me! No one else had, apparently, but after that, I believed.

I met my husband Jon through the matchmaking efforts of my priest and his wife. We both resisted. Each of us loved our church and neither wanted to risk losing it over a failed personal relationship! Nevertheless, Jon and I met and those two were right. We recently celebrated twenty-one years together.

Marrying Jon meant an instant family, a blessing and a challenge. Jon had full custody of his twelve-year-old son Scott, an epileptic with many developmental delays and learning disabilities. Unlike many similarly challenged kids, Scott looked normal—in fact, he was a very handsome young man—which made other people's expectations higher and made it more frustrating for Scott to accept his limitations, both heartbreaking circumstances. We couldn't leave him alone or with just anyone, and his mother had completely abandoned him. Not an easy situation for two newlyweds.

Scott struggled through school in special education classes. Jon devoted himself to his son, tutoring him academically and teaching him basic life skills. Jon became trained in special education, and served as an aide in the classroom. At eighteen, Scott was accepted into a state run "Independent Living

Skills" home where he learned to cook, do laundry, pay bills, take the bus and hold a job. Scott graduated from this home-based training program, moved into a supervised house with another graduate, and landed the job of his dreams—as a clerk at Blockbuster Video! Scott was so happy! He had made it! It was the pinnacle of Jon's and Scott's hard work and determination. We were so proud!

A few short years later, at twenty-two, Scott was dead. He'd died in the shower of a suspected brain aneurism. There'd been no warnings. I will never forget the shock, the disbelief I felt when they came to tell us. By this time, Jon and I had two more children, boys ages 4 and 2, who played blissfully in the yard while inside we broke down at the news. How and why did this happen? We couldn't make sense of it. "I've wasted my life," mourned Jon. "I've worked so hard to enable Scott to make his way in this world, and now, for what?"

The following day, a Sunday, we attended church. During the peace offering, we held fast to one another and cried. Our church family surrounded us and prayed with us. We found things to be thankful for: that Scott's passing was quick and painless; that he had not suffered a long, painful battle with cancer, as his cousin had; that he was not killed by a drunk driver, which would have left us seething in anger. Still, it wasn't easy.

Scott's funeral filled the church. Jon spoke from his heart. He thanked Scott's young video store colleagues for going out of their way to include Scott, at work and socially. He thanked Scott's church friends, especially the young ladies who danced with him at parties. There is an African proverb, "It takes a village to raise a child." Never is this truer than in raising a special needs child. At some point, even the unwavering attention and dedication of loving parents are not enough. The caring teens and young adults in his life had become a vital part of Scott's village.

One friend lost her son to an allergic reaction. He'd died alone in a hotel room. When Scott died, she said simply, 'I know how you feel.' Just like joy, we must share pain. It is in the sharing, for me, that God's grace eases the pain. When I share joy or pain with those I love, I know I've either raised them up, or they've raised me up. When someone shares their pain with me, I take a little of it from them. I pray for them, for their situation, for God's blessing in their lives. When I share my pain with someone, I don't feel so alone. I know they pray for me, and it helps.

Nothing can prepare a parent for losing a child. Even with the passage of time, there is no "reason" that makes sense. The only hopeful response is to piece one's life back together, built on a foundation of what matters most. For Jon, years of dedicated, patient parenting to Scott prepared him to father two young sons as an older parent. One reason we'd decided to have more children was to ensure that Scott would have family to care for him after we were gone. Yet in the aftermath of losing Scott, I thank God we had our two boys for us—they gave us a reason to rebuild our lives. We focused on them, centered on what mattered most: our family and our faith. For me, the hardest part about losing Scott was not being able to say goodbye and to tell him I loved him, one more time. Jon and I are both very aware of this, and make a point to count our blessings daily and let those around us know we care.

Losing Scott was a major storm in our lives, but there was more to come.

At 46, when my sons were only 10 and 8, I was diagnosed with Multiple Sclerosis (MS), an incurable, progressive nervous system disease, shedding a whole new light on the depression and exhaustion I'd experienced after my divorce twenty years ago. My younger sister Nancy had been diagnosed fifteen years earlier, so I thought I "knew" what MS entailed. Because of her diagnosis, I researched MS, joined support groups and did everything I could to help Nancy cope. Even so, when I experienced its painful and debilitating symptoms myself, it shook my world. I stumbled and fell down often. I couldn't see. I had a severe reaction to the medication. I had no energy. I was the family breadwinner; what would happen to us? I remember asking Jon, "Am I going to die?" So much for being informed . . . little comfort that brought me!

The first twenty months after the diagnosis were the worst, mostly due to the medication I was prescribed. At best, medications may slow down or curtail symptoms, but they can't repair damage or cure the disease. Prescribing the right medication is difficult, as MS affects everyone differently. Sometimes the side effects of medication are worse than the symptoms of the disease. It can be a long process of trial and error.

Once my symptoms were under control, I felt much better. I researched MS and joined support groups with a whole new vigor, even helping my sister in the process. When Nancy was diagnosed, the general consensus was dismal, basically, "Buy a wheelchair and prepare to die." When I told Nancy that I had MS, she wept. But MS is not a death sentence. Nancy and I openly talk about MS in a way now that we never could before. We share embarrassing incidents, funny falls, medicine advice, injection ideas, mobility aids, etc. It's good that we have each other. We laugh and cry together. I know that through God's will, I have helped her and others cope with and manage this disease. I belong to a support group, and we help each other and educate our community.

When I was first diagnosed, a priest from my church offered to do a healing service. I told him that I didn't need to be 'healed of MS.' As strange as it sounds, I feel that God is using me and my MS to reach out to others. Instead of healing me of MS, I asked the priest to pray for God's continued blessing in showing me how to *use my MS to help others,* whether they suffered from this particular disease or not. We had the service, though I don't think he ever 'got it.'

MS is part of me and it affects how I live my life, but it is not who I am. I am still a Type A personality with big ideas of what I can accomplish. But through MS, I have learned to slow down, pay attention, and to be more compassionate and helpful to others. I have been blessed with a good, long-term, stable job that pays well and provides benefits. Because of that, Jon has been able to stay home with the boys though he continues to work and volunteer as a special education aide. Our marriage partnership works, even if it looks like role reversal to many.

We made changes in our lives to accommodate my physical challenges. We moved closer to my job, so that I could conserve commute time, energy and strength and could come home to rest at lunch. In the process, we downsized our home and yard to make it easier to maintain.

I am open about my MS, even at work. I sell specialty lumber products, a male-dominated industry, and I continue to perform well. In fact, my candor about my MS, and my willingness to listen and show concern for others, has been a form of 'free agent ministry in the workplace.' My open nature in the face of my diagnosis gives work colleagues permission to share their fears candidly with me, and for me to pray for them. I wear a cross that signifies that I am Christian. It reminds *me* of who I am. Like my mother, I am open and vocal about my

Christianity. I never push my religion on anyone. God does not live in a building called church or in a single denomination called Episcopalian. God lives in acts of kindness, of genuine caring, of humble prayer or service.

MS is not something 'wrong' with me; instead it's a vehicle through which I can do God's work in a way that I couldn't, if I didn't have it. I believe that God is using me, and this condition, to help others. Rather than feeling punished by it, I feel MS is a gift and a blessing. It humbles me and slows me down enough to do God's will—which I believe is to love people, and to be there for them. My life has gotten better, in the ways that matter most. My family, faith and friendships are enriched and uplifted. No matter what, life is good, and joy is available to all of us . . . no matter what.

Sally offered the following spiritual advice to help others who suffer, whether it is a chronic medical condition, or the loss of a child:

1. Pray daily. Never give up trying to *connect* with Christ (or the God of your understanding.)

2. Take *everything* to God, with no exception—the good, the bad, the ugly, the terrifying, and the joyful.

3. Remember that you're never alone, God is always with you.

4. Share yourself, *your challenges and gifts* with others. We're all in this together.

CHAPTER TWO

Naomi

(Written by Susan O'Shaugnessy)

What does it mean to say good-bye to your husband, soul mate, travel companion and business partner? How does it affect your faith and spiritual practices? How do you rebuild a meaningful life?

After 41 years of marriage, it's not surprising that Naomi had a hard time saying goodbye to her beloved husband, Luc. And they weren't simply years ticked off on a calendar, but rich ones, filled with intimate traditions and small and large tokens of love. Even today, Naomi looks down from her second-story home office to a gentle, heart-shaped set of grey stones that surround a small copse of ferns in her garden. Luc placed these stones as one of the weekly "Friday Gifts" they exchanged through their marriage.

They met on Christmas Day, 1963, in his mother's living room. She was nineteen, a college student; he was twenty-six, preparing to leave the military. Although they were both raised in traditional Black Christian churches—she, Baptist and he, Episcopalian—they both believed in non-traditional concepts of spirituality. After their first meeting, they discussed these ideas during daily phone conversations.

"For the first three weeks we could only talk on the phone. I was studying for finals, and Dad wouldn't let me date. We talked for hours, and we found that we had a lot in common. Not that we liked the same books or movies or music. Luc listened to classical music; he liked Shostakovich. I couldn't even spell that name. I loved Smokey Robinson and the Miracles. It wasn't things of the world we had in common; we shared things of the mind and spirit. All of our belief systems were so similar.

"For example, we both believed in reincarnation—that these are rent-a-bodies, and each time you go out in death and come back in rebirth, you are either destined to repeat the lessons you didn't learn or you ascend to the next level of spirituality. So life is eternal, but these rental units wear out. Those are the kinds of conversations we would have. And those are the things we shared deeply in common."

So they got married and built a life together. They traveled and even worked together after she launched a successful business, and he helped as her second-in-command. They maintained a strict, respectful code of conduct: never badmouth your spouse to other people, always tell the truth to each other—even if it makes you look bad, and never make unilateral decisions.

Of course, the better the partnership, the harder it is to let it go. In January 2005, Luc caught a cold that he couldn't shake and that sapped his energy, highly uncharacteristic for the vibrant sixty-eight year old most people mistook for a man in his fifties. Luc maintained a healthy lifestyle, working out regularly and running frequent marathons. He shunned red meat and hard liquor, ate lots of vegetables and little sugar. Nonetheless, Luc was diagnosed with pancreatic cancer on March 30, and he died a mere 33 days later.

"Luc was not afraid to die," Naomi recalls. "He said his life was complete. He had done everything he wanted to do: fly a plane, learn French, live in Paris, travel to places he saw in National Geographic, love wisely, drink wine and enjoy life. His only regret was leaving me."

Another reason Luc was not afraid to die was that he had done it once before, thirty years ago, leaving Naomi a widow for four hours during a vacation in Spain. While horseback riding, Luc inadvertently disturbed a hornets' nest and was stung over fifty times. Naomi struggled to make him comfortable, but he became increasingly ill, ultimately losing consciousness. Naomi summoned help from an American nurse renting the condo next door. When they couldn't rouse him, Naomi called a Spanish doctor. In shock, she watched the doctor pull the green-striped bed sheet over Luc's face. "*Su esposo es muerte,*" he said. ("Your husband is dead.")

Numb, head spinning, Naomi spent hours with the doctor, completing paperwork, making plans for the body, concentrating on the monumental tasks ahead to keep from succumbing to grief. She worried about when she should call their parents given the six-hour time difference, which made it practically the middle of the night in the States. She decided to wait until after 7 a.m. U.S. time and remains grateful she did.

"It was so bizarre. Luc suddenly sat up in bed. The sheet fell from his face, and he said, 'Man, I'm really hungry.' The doctor made the sign of the cross, backed out of the room, and drove away. He didn't even examine Luc. I screamed. I was hysterical. It took me a while to believe he was really back and not some zombie. His face was clear. He was fine."

When examined by doctors back home, Luc showed multiple signs of a massive stroke, including a tell-tale lightning bolt shaped lesion on the CAT scan. The neurologists couldn't explain it. "They told us that with that much damage, Luc should be dead or at the very least, highly diminished in capacity," Naomi recalls. "Luc just smiled and said, 'Guess it wasn't my time yet.'"

When he eventually remembered details of his near-death experience, Luc described it as beautiful and peaceful, bearing marked similarities to other documented cases, though he'd never read any of them.

"Luc said the whole time he was dead, he wasn't in the room. He was in the light. He said he couldn't describe it in words, but that it was like being embraced by a beautiful light and hearing beautiful music. He was asked the question, 'Are you done? Are you ready to go?' When he said 'no,' then *boom*, he came back into his body. That's when he sat up."

Naomi relied on this memory during Luc's last days. "I held the Spain experience with me during his final illness. I sat with him at the hospital for an hour after he died, and I told the funeral home to wait three days before they embalmed him—just in case he decided to wake up and rejoin me."

But Luc's diagnosis was severe from the beginning, and neither of them relied on false hopes. "We talked about death during his illness in many ways. I told him he needed to continue on his own journey. We were both clear that this was not our first time together in this world. We'd been here before as partners—maybe as brother and sister, or teacher and student. And we knew this was not our last time. In the reincarnation cycle, we are connected. I'll see him again.

"Of course I miss him, but I know that he's OK. In fact, he's better off than I am. He's up there partying with people like Christopher Reeve, Richard Pryor, Luther Vandross,

Coretta Scott King and Rosa Parks. He's having such a good time. And I'm bored down here with all these mortal people!" Naomi laughs, her sense of humor intact.

"Before he died, he told me that he would look out for me, and I still feel his presence. Stuff has happened since he's been gone that I can only chalk up to the Spirit world. For example, there's a manually activated fan that occasionally turns on by itself while I'm in the kitchen. Other times, the intercom rings from his office. I pick it up and don't hear anything. I guess it's a 1-800 call from heaven. He's letting me know that he's here.

"On a recent trip to Egypt, I had a chance to sit in silence and meditate inside the Great Pyramid near Cairo. At one point, I had a vision of Luc sitting in front of me, reaching out his hands to hold mine. I opened my eyes and 'saw' him there, in a favorite plaid shirt and black jeans, smiling at me. I reached out my hands and felt him touch me. Yes, I cried, but they were tears of joy at seeing him again."

Even with these signs and her own spiritual awareness, Naomi endures the classic stages of grief, moving in and out of myriad feelings, such as denial, anger and sadness.

"I'll go into denial for several moments. I'll tell myself, 'He's just gone on a business trip. When I get home tonight, he'll be there.' And part of me believes that's true. Then I realize it's just a story I'm making up. Sometimes I'll experience anger. Like I when I'm trying to figure out some electronic gadget, and it took me a really long time, and I was thinking 'darn it, if he were here, this would be really quick.' Luc was so good at that stuff. I'm angry that he's not here. Other times, I'm sad for no reason. It's related to the grief, but I can't quite label it.

"I thought that I would move through the stages of grief

and check them off like a to-do list. So when the same stage came around again, I would get frustrated. 'I did this already!' But I've realized I'm moving through them at different levels. I understand now that I'll go through these stages for a long time. When something I've dealt with before comes up again, I honor it, but I don't give it a lot of energy or beat myself up over it. I note the stage and move forward."

While grieving, Naomi has found concrete ways to honor Luc's memory. The spring after he died, she invited friends over to plant a garden Luc had secretly designed as a surprise for their forty-second anniversary. Sitting in her backyard today, she is surrounded by the sights and scents of plants and flowers Luc loved. She's added a few touches of her own, too, like old cathedral window frames hung to one side, and a wrought iron railing and candleholder. "Our combined plans bring me such peace and make me feel like I'm in both a garden and a church."

It's a lovely image but also a reflection of her healing journey. "Focus on what you've found rather than on what you've lost. I could live in the land of loss. I lost my husband, my business partner, my traveling companion, my soul mate—the list goes on and on. And I've seen women live there. They carry their dead husbands around like albatrosses, seeking sympathy and comfort from people long after he's gone. I don't mean ignore the loss; it's significant. But do not move in and buy a condo. Live in the land of what could be, in the here and now. It's far more interesting. Talk about your grief only with a few like-minded people, rather than parading it as a banner for pity.

"As much as you can, use the opportunity to learn and grow, to explore your own strength. Many women, myself included, leaned on husbands for strength they didn't believe they had. I had to learn to do more things independently. It took me six hours to program the GPS system in our SUV. He could've done it in six minutes. I'm still working on the digital recording system on our bedroom TV. I'm at sixteen hours. I'll get back to you on that one. I may need to call for help soon!"

Finally, Naomi reminds us to be conscious of the journey, our emotions in the process, and to trust and honor them. "Be one-hundred percent of what you're feeling. Do not act the way people think you should. Friends and family thought I shouldn't go back to work so soon. Yes, I was sad and bereft, but I have a business, and I need to make payroll and pay for my house and for the funeral. Crying at home alone while sorting Luc's clothes would not generate billable hours.

"People also thought that I should've had a viewing for his funeral. I'm sorry, if you can't remember what he looked like when he was living, then you're not going to see him dead. It might be a harsh position, but it's one I felt strongly about."

Naomi trusted herself to do what was right for her and her grief. In place of a traditional funeral, Naomi chose to have a celebration service to honor Luc's life. The gathering included people of all ages and races; the mood was a mixture of joy and loss. Pictures of Luc's garden flowers were projected on the sanctuary wall, and his best friend ran a slide show of their times together. One at a time, friends and family shared stories and memories of Luc, painting a picture of a man who lived with verve, insisted on thinking independently and wouldn't be deterred by the prejudice of others.

When Georgia, a new friend of Luc's, stood up to share her memories, she put her hands on her hips and said: "I'm a little annoyed by all this sharing. I thought I had a special relationship with Luc and that he only talked to me about life this way. Now I find out he had that relationship with everyone." Georgia smiled. "Well, it was still special and I will always cherish it."

Naomi continues to honor the events that she and Luc celebrated together, such as his birthday and their anniversary. She even sends herself flowers and signs Luc's name. "When I get them, I say 'Oh honey, thanks. Those are just the kind I wanted.'"

Spiritual practice has also become a more central part of Naomi's life. She's started *A Course in Miracles,* a curriculum of universal spiritual themes that focuses on reframing how you view people and situations. She attends weekly discussion groups, studies the daily lesson and meditates.

"Since Luc's death, I have become more in touch with Spirit. Before that, it was a conversation, an occasional experience, a belief system, but also slightly abstract. Death is a wake-up call. And that's why I think Luc's death was a gift. The only important thing for me to focus on today and for the rest of my life is, 'What is the lesson I need to learn, and what do I need to pass on to somebody else?' That's all."

"When somebody dies, it strips us down to the core. In the weeks that follow, nothing is important: bill paying, a job, gas in the car. These things are meaningless. You get real clear about what's important in life and it's not any of the stuff. It's the basic principles of living. Death is a reminder to attend to what is truly important in life and not get caught up in material things and useless beliefs that don't forward the universe."

Naomi reflects on her 41-year marriage and on Luc's absence as she looks out at their garden. "Life is eternal. Luc is just a little further up the road, around the bend. He's here, I just can't see him. But if I look hard, I can just see the edge of his plaid shirt."

CHAPTER THREE

Ellen

I was raised in a conservative Jewish home, in a Jewish New Jersey community. Growing up, it felt like everyone was Jewish. I took the rhythm of the rituals for granted. We attended synagogue, celebrated Shabbats (Sabbath) every Friday night, lit candles and recited traditional Jewish prayers. We celebrated the holy days. I never gave it a second thought. As I moved away to college and began my life as a single adult, I allowed my Jewish practice to lapse.

Even so, I took the values and lessons of my upbringing into adulthood. I can't overstate the depth and breadth of my parents' love and their impact in my life. By their example, I learned life is meant to live. They were so full of vim and vigor, always looking for the positive spin in a situation. They found joy in the simplest moments. Their lives weren't easy, but you would have never known it by watching them. My grandmothers were both bitter and negative people, but I never heard either of my parents complain about their childhoods. My father was a flight navigator shot down in WWII, a Jewish POW held in Germany for eleven months. He never once spoke of his hardship or his fear.

I was very close to my parents. They meant everything to me. My mom died at sixty-nine, after fifteen years of rectal cancer, undergoing extensive surgery, treatment, rehabilitation and chemotherapy. I traveled often to visit her, and we had the gift of a long sweet goodbye, an opportunity to serve her and to live the Jewish principle, "we value life above all." She was a wonderful, kind, loving mother and wife and my father devoted himself to caring for her through her years of decline. He did everything with such tenderness and love, bathing, dressing, and feeding her. His kind, steadfast example made a huge impression on me.

My mother died on a Saturday, and I flew back to New Jersey from my home in Salt Lake City for the Tuesday funeral. My husband Edd and my sixteen-year-old stepson James joined me, though they flew back to Utah the next day. I stayed with my father to sit *shiva*, a Jewish custom of mourning and celebrating the life of a loved one for seven days after the death during which the family sits together, rests, and welcomes relatives and friends into their home, while the friends and relatives honor the death through gifts of food and service to the family.

Two days after the service, a good friend came to me with the news that I had to call home immediately. I could tell something dreadful had happened, but I was shocked when Edd answered the phone to tell me, choked and sobbing, that James had shot himself with a rifle to the head. He was dead.

Still reeling from my mother's death, I could hardly absorb the news. Nonetheless, I was touched and humbled when my father announced without hesitation he would fly back with me to be there for us. During the flight through Dallas, we were both moved when Delta airlines staff waited with us during the stopover, offering condolences to us and sending support to Edd, a Delta pilot.

Close friends met us and took us home, and we arrived to find the barn where James had killed himself cleaned, all evidence of the grim event erased by kind neighbors. It was a first, symbolic step toward getting our lives back in order, but we had a long journey ahead of us.

There is no way to describe how shattered we felt. James had been seeing a therapist, but none of us felt he was dealing with anything other than usual teenage challenges. We visited the therapist every day for two weeks after James died. In a daze, we cried, we agonized, and we began the tortured process of studying the puzzle pieces. We strained to see patterns, connections and trends in James' behavior and thoughts. Nothing remotely hinted that he was considering such a drastic action. We would pore over the pieces for years, looking for a hidden clue or sign of what was going on in James' mind that would lead him to take his own life. We found nothing.

After the funeral, when flowers wilted, and sympathy cards no longer arrived, we experienced a dark abyss of grief. What now? I consumed every book I could find on suicide, trying in vain to grasp what had happened. I especially related to the book *My Son, My Son,* by Iris Bolton, a trained psychotherapist and active community social worker whose own son took his life without warning, leaving her reeling and full of unanswered questions. Convinced I was a good stepmom to James, that I was intimately involved in every detail of his life, that I was there every day after school with milk and cookies and homework help—the June Cleaver story, Jewish style—I couldn't fathom how he could do such a thing and why I hadn't seen it coming.

You wrestle with the details, over and over, until it exhausts you. Stare at the puzzle pieces; move them around endlessly in your mind, review, review, and more review. Still no picture forms, no conclusion can be drawn, but not for lack of effort. You stop for a while, catch your breath, tell yourself you can't change it, it's over, let go. For a while you allow yourself a sweet respite. But one day you get an urge to look again, and even though you know it's not healthy, you can't help yourself. You stare at and study the puzzle pieces again.

It's an endless, exhausting cycle with no answers. WHY? Parents of suicide victims never stop asking themselves, torturing themselves, with that question. We're convinced we've failed our children, that we did something to drive them to it, or we didn't protect or nurture them enough. It's fruitless, of course, but that doesn't stop us. It's one of the great tragedies of suicide—so many people feel responsible, yet in most cases, no one's at fault. And the only person with any real answers isn't around to give them.

Edd and I took one positive, deliberate step soon after the funeral. We met with James' closest friends, his ecumenical Boy Scout troop who had bravely worn their uniforms and carried the flag at his service. We were committed to these boys, and determined to muster the strength to invest in their safety and emotional well-being. To us, they represented James at his best, and what remained.

We called them together and told them, "There are no questions that can't be asked today. We'll do our best to be open, honest and forthright with you, and we will ask that you do the same with us." We were worried that James' suicide might spark "copy cat" behavior, a misplaced glory of grieving, or that the more emotionally fragile boys might plunge into a tailspin over James' suicide. These boys' survival was critical to our progress. Suicide in 1995 was (and remains today) a leading cause of teenage death with a strong, associated stigma. At the time, kids had nowhere to turn to get their toughest questions answered.

Their questions were innocent, naïve, open and honest and the meeting lasted for hours. Edd and I decided beforehand to be honest with the boys and to demonstrate our resolve to embrace life fully (though we had no idea how at this early stage of grief), and to be completely nonjudgmental. We did our best to answer truthfully and hopefully:

"What are you going to do with James' things?" (Such a teenage question, when one's emerging identity is closely aligned with stuff. We told them we would sort through James' things when we felt ready. Eventually we gave most of his treasured items to his younger sister, and some to his closest friends.)

"Were you surprised that he did this?" (Surprised? No, more like shocked and devastated.)

"Why did he do it?" (We don't know, but please, if any of you start feeling desperate or sad like James must have felt, seek help from your parents or other caring, responsible adults immediately.)

"Can we talk about him with you and with each other when you're around?" (Yes, please, please, please. The sound of his name is music to our ears.)

"How are you doing? Are you OK?" (We were touched by their concern for us, and how they identified how their own parents would react in similar circumstances. No, we're not OK right now, but we will be someday.)

Thank God for these boys; they gave us a reason to not give up. The meeting proved to be an important step in all of our healing. Some of them felt responsible in some way, that something they did or didn't do led to James' actions, but we reassured them all that what James did was no one's fault, that he had acted on his own and that we would never understand what he was thinking at the time—an important reminder for ourselves, as well.

To this day, these young men remain in our lives. We attend their weddings, graduation parties and other special occasions. One of the boys close to James told me years later that he'd considered suicide in a very low moment, but remembering the pain that James' action had caused us and his friends stopped him.

Time passed. Edd went back to work. I knew his heart was shattered, but he was functioning, and showing up for a structured, demanding job that he enjoyed, surrounded by supportive friends and colleagues, helped him. I had retired from corporate life four years before, when James came to live with us. Home alone, without a purpose, nurturing no one, I realized I would never be in a position to nurture and support anyone else, if I didn't first nurture myself.

I am blessed with passion and a love for life and I knew I would need to re-engage, and part of that was processing these recent tragedies. I worked hard at grieving, the hardest I have ever worked at anything in my life. Along the way I began to pray daily, and often throughout the day, especially when emotional darkness set in. I re-discovered the comfort, familiarity, and strength of traditional Jewish ritual. In my darkest moments, I took comfort in repeating the prayers, lighting the candles and attending synagogue on holy days. It helped me remember who I was, and where I came from. Reconnecting with the Jewish community nurtured me and helped me feel at home in Salt Lake City.

I attended individual therapy and support groups for suicide survivors. I sought medical help for depression, and took medication to help me endure the difficult months following James' and my mom's deaths. I became a voracious consumer of books on suicide. I left no rock unturned. I felt like I was in a fight for my own life, and I was completely devoted to the cause.

My first inkling of healing and hope came almost two years after James' death. I joined a book club. I know that it doesn't sound like much, but at the time, it felt like an enormous undertaking. I committed to reading an entire book, cover-to-cover, unrelated to grief, once a month and to show up at a meeting to discuss it. It was my first step in re-engaging in life beyond James' suicide. It might have looked insignificant to others, but it was huge forward step in my own recovery.

About that same time, I made the unwelcome discovery that I was a "grief junkie," a sympathy gatherer, telling and retelling my story of James so it had come to define me. I'd become stuck in it, so that my experience of life and others' experience of me revolved around that event. And I'm a little ashamed to admit that I think sometimes I liked that, I liked the drama and the shock-value, and the way people reacted to me when I told them.

Don't get me wrong. The story is true, of course; it did happen. James' suicide changed me at depth; I will never be the same person I was before his death. But this loss, however tragic and life altering, is not who I am, and at that time, it started to become who I was. I made the important choice to make the story about helping other people, rather than using it as a springboard for sympathy or attention.

Today, I only tell the story of James if I think it will serve another person, to help someone who has lost a child. I no longer tell the story for me, but to establish trust and empathy, as someone who has survived the same experience. And then I encourage them to tell their story and I listen attentively. I see my role as a loving witness for them, not as a storyteller who merely waits her turn to exchange her story for theirs. There is a huge difference, and I understand that so clearly now.

Once I established to myself that true healing was my own personal priority, rather than dwelling in the story of my tragic experiences, I continued to look for ways to help the process. As I mentioned, I turned even more fully to faith rituals I'd learned in my childhood, bringing me deeper and more fully into a spiritual connection as well as a Jewish community.

I was blessed with good friends who showed up for me in big and small ways, even when I was too numb to let them know I'd noticed. They supported me with food, hugs, walks, and invitations to literally cry on their shoulders. They checked in on me when Edd was flying, so I wouldn't be alone or feel isolated. They encouraged, nagged and supported me to nurture myself, physically, mentally, emotionally and spiritually. They never gave up on me, and I am so grateful.

I've had some real medical challenges through my adult life, and I think this, too, made me realize how important it was to take care of myself as much as I possibly could. Before my marriage, when faced with medical hurdles, my father and mother were always there for me. They didn't have much money, but they knew how to be there for me when I was weak and afraid. And then later, Edd showered me with the same kind of tender, loving care through my recovery periods. I'm so grateful that I married a man as loyal and committed as Edd. Through these two men, I learned how important care really was, especially during a crisis. I used their example in my own healing process, devoting myself to my health, my own self-care.

Physical exercise was critical, especially when I had so little energy and strength. Getting out of bed to do something, anything, was a modest commitment to my own health, mental, physical and spiritual. Just moving my body became an essential habit toward recovery, a vital necessity for staying engaged. One step of my foot meant one step closer to healing.

My final step was the moment I realized I needed to redefine my purpose. I decided to be a resource for others, rather than a princess at her own pity party. I'd fallen into a trap of feeling sorry for myself, and I needed to climb out of it and find some way to serve. My dad did that for me after my mother died; it was time to become the daughter my parents had raised me to be.

I volunteered for the Susan G. Komen Race for the Cure®, a nonprofit organization that raises money to promote breast cancer research, education, screening and treatment. Over the past eight years I've served the local affiliate in a number of ways, including serving on the Board of Directors and chairing the Salt Lake City Race for the Cure®, an enormous undertaking which includes over fifteen thousand participants and earns hundreds of thousands of dollars.

I chose Race for the Cure® because it's always scheduled on Mother's Day weekend, an emotionally significant time for me. Rather than spending every Mother's Day mourning my mother and my stepson, the Race gives me a focus and a cause, not to mention a disciplined, demanding schedule. The race is both distracting and fulfilling.

A side-lesson, one that I would give almost anything not to have learned, is that not everyone can be there for you in the ways you'd like them to be, especially in what they say to you. There you are in the early days of grief, struggling to simply get out of bed in the morning, and you have to face insensitive, hurtful questions and situations.

"So, did you ever figure out why James took his life?" I wish I could teach people not to ask or say stupid things. It's one of the ironies of suffering a great loss. You hope you never said the same stupid things, before you knew better. Now you know to keep it simple, kind, and nonjudgmental. "I'm so sorry," suffices. So does, "This is hard, I'm sorry." Just make them feel loved and supported; help them nourish their body, heart and soul as they nurse their wounds. What they'll remember for many years is not what you said, but how you made them feel.

And sometimes well-meaning, religious friends can drain energy from you with their prosaic, catch-all phrases and judgments. I had a good friend who, just 6 months after James and my mom died, asked me if I ever went a whole day without thinking of them, implying I would be much happier if I could just "get over it" and get on with my life. I thought, "I feel like it is a personal victory if I can go a single hour without sinking to my knees in pain. *A WHOLE DAY?* What is she thinking?"

She chastised me that my faith in God was insufficient and by now (all of 6 months later!) I should be moving on. If James had died, it was all part of God's plan, and I should be at peace with that. This really hurt. How dare she prescribe my grief, or judge me for it? I wanted to scream back, "Excuse me, I'm grieving as fast as I can!" But I didn't.

The exchange strained our long friendship, and on Yom Kippur, the Jewish holy day when we are called to make amends for things we've done that may have hurt another, I wrote her a note asking for her forgiveness for anything I'd done to offend her. She wrote back saying that if I genuinely cared for her, I would never write again.

Life doesn't unfold within a tidy box that fits our expectations, plans or timetables, or even our religious beliefs. It just unfolds, sometimes by chance, sometimes by choice, and often by a combination of the two in a wild, unpredictable fashion. There's no such thing as "my fair share of suffering." Life happens, unaffected by your rules or my rules. You deal with it the best that you can. I completely abandoned any illusion that I had control over people and things. We can't make others understand or love us, let alone forgive us.

James' suicide was not in my life plan, but I can't argue with the reality that he is dead. Some would say he died too soon, it was not his time, or he lived an incomplete life. Who am I to say? If you believe in God, then apparently it was his time. His life plan according to God was to live 16 years, 7 months, no more and no less. Sometimes I recycle back through the stages of grief, back to ground zero of denial, anger, shock, disbelief, bargaining and finally I rediscover acceptance again. You don't go through the grief cycle once, but many times. Often an event, a memory, a song or an aroma retriggers the cycle when you least expect it. But over the years, the pain gets less intense, and lasts less time than in the early years. I've learned to hang on, to nurture myself, especially when acute grief revisits.

Above all, I am so grateful for the principles and practices my parents instilled in me. My father is now deceased, so on Yom Kippur and on their Yahrzeit (the anniversary of their deaths) I recite Kaddish, the Jewish prayer for the deceased for both of them. It helps me remember who they were, what they stood for, and that it's important to carry on their legacies. I give charity in their name, a Jewish custom that honors the memory of loved ones by making a positive impact in the here and now. I still ask them for advice and direction when something troubles me.

My father remained kind, gentle, and caring all the days of his life. When I once asked him how I would ever cope with losing him, he answered, "Truly Ellen, I won't be very far way." Such was his faith. Now it's my job to carry on our family legacy and to embrace life, to embrace all of life, the sorrows and the tragedies as well as the joys.

So goes the traditional Jewish toast: "L'Chaim—to life!"

CHAPTER FOUR

Mariam

Ramadan, the ninth month of the Arabic calendar during which the Q'uran was revealed to Mohammed, is celebrated by Muslims throughout the world. For the entire month, Muslims fast during the daylight hours and in the evening eat small meals and visit with friends and family. It is a time of worship and contemplation. A time to strengthen family and community ties.

This religious fasting is a symbol of sacrifice and purification, a measure of self-restraint, and a yearly lesson in humility and patience, encouraging compassion for those less fortunate. Charity and service are particularly emphasized during Ramadan, and Muslims are required to donate food and a percentage of their wealth to the poor.

During this holy month, Mariam is the portrait of a devout Muslim woman. Asking her about it, one understands her commitment to study, pray and reflect, to open herself up to Allah (the Muslim word for God), and listen with grace and discernment for guidance, strength and clarity.

But this graceful, devoted, disciplined practice comes at

the end of a long, twisting, difficult road, one that begins and ends with Islam, but swings through hardship, pain and doubt:

I took religion, Islam, for granted. I was raised in Damascus, Syria, a predominately Muslim society. It's hard to say where Islam began, and Middle Eastern culture left off. Religion and culture were highly integrated, almost seamless. Everyone I knew was Muslim. I was not raised a religious person per se, but prayer, kindness, and charity were my parents' daily practice. They were shining examples of the Prophet Muhammad's mercy in action, always taking care of friends, neighbors or anyone needing help.

My father was a shopkeeper, my mother a seamstress. When I was a child in Syria, you couldn't buy clothes off racks in the store, like you can now. My mother bought fabric and sewed everything, for us, our friends, even a family of children left orphaned. She never accepted or expected anything for what she made. Beyond that, my parents never even mentioned their good deeds. So my understanding of what the Prophet taught us embraced the sincerity and humility of doing good works, not just whether we prayed five times a day and fasted during the appropriate times. And I suppose I neglected the more disciplined aspects of my religion.

When I was 18, I married a promising young man from a wealthy, Jordanian family. It was an arranged marriage, as was the custom, and it thrust me into a fast life —international travel, high society, servants, *haute couture,* the whole bit. It was a whirlwind, a teen-age girl's dream, and at first, I was thrilled.

After a while, though, I learned that a party can only last so long, and no material luxuries could replace what I needed most: support, help, and a husband who didn't drink or abuse me.

Less than ten years into the marriage, we had three sons. My husband traveled frequently, for long periods of time, which helped me cope with my increasingly difficult, lonely marriage. As a dutiful Muslim wife, I tried to accept his behavior with patience and tolerance. Divorce, although legally permissible within our religion, was very rare forty years ago. I didn't know anything about alcoholism; Alcoholics Anonymous and marriage counseling didn't exist, at least in the Middle East, and even if it did, I'm not sure I would have known how to ask for help. I was even ashamed to tell my parents.

My husband's conduct grew more outrageous and erratic. Of course now I know how classic the story is, alcoholism and violence. But at the time, I had no idea what to do or where to turn. Without warning, he would shift dramatically from gentle kindness to intense anger. It was a living hell; I never knew what to expect. Sometimes when he drank and lashed out, I would hide in the bathtub overnight, hoping for safety until he came back to his senses. Mornings after such episodes, he would beg for forgiveness and promise to change, but he never did.

I focused all of my attention on my children, but it became harder and harder to pretend nothing was wrong, no matter how good things seemed to the world outside. The day before my youngest son Marwan's first birthday I went to the doctor. We were living in Dubai, and my two older sons were away at boarding school in Europe. Despondent, I confessed to my doctor, a neighbor and friend, that I felt fatigued and depressed. He ran a blood test and informed me with delight that I was pregnant!

I broke out in tears, sobbing in his office.

My reaction astounded and baffled him. "Isn't this glorious news?"

Of course it wasn't. I broke down and told him of my troubled marriage, my husband's drinking and violence, my concern for my children and myself. How could I bring yet another child into this chaos, hopelessness and despair? My doctor didn't know how to respond. He comforted me, but my heart-wrenching revelations put him in an awkward position. This was a man we socialized with, and my problems felt like dirty laundry.

Returning home, I felt even more vulnerable and hopeless, but I tried to pull myself together to celebrate my baby's birthday the next day. That very evening, Marwan tried to climb into his crib and fell backward, hitting his head on the floor. Hours later, he was dead.

This was the darkest day of my life, but also, I think, the turning point.

I cried hysterically for hours; I couldn't stop. Inconsolable, I felt like I couldn't go on. My best friend tried to comfort me and, worried for my safety, summoned a man known for his wisdom and piety.

To this day, I'm not completely sure what this man's name was or what he said to me, but I believe he saved my life. And I know he reawakened my spiritual awareness.

His wise, calm presence soothed me. He talked to me for hours and hours. He reminded me of the eternal nature of life and reassured me that, some day, God willing, Marwan would act as my intercessor, welcoming me to heaven. He read from the Q'uran. He shared stories of healing and redemption from his own experience and from the Prophet's lifetime. His voice, his manner, his willingness to sit with me—all of these things touched me, comforted my distress.

Slowly, my hysterical sobbing mellowed to quiet tears. My broken heart mended, ever so slightly. Deep within, something stirred. God's voice spoke to me, and for the first time in a very long while, I listened.

After Marwan's funeral, I asked my husband for a divorce, but he convinced me to give him a second chance. As I mentioned, divorce among Muslim couples was nearly nonexistent and even more rarely requested by the wife. We were both aware of the social stigma a divorce would give us. He truly loved me, and when he was sober, rational and clear-headed, he was a good, gentle man. He promised me he would work to control his drinking and would never again threaten or bully me.

He kept his word, at least for a while. Our daughter, Leila, the new love of my life, was born, but soon afterwards, my husband fell back into his excessive drinking and erratic behavior. Looking back, I believe he sincerely wanted to change, but neither of us knew how to make it happen. He needed professional help, but that wasn't the way of the times, and I don't think he ever would have asked for it.

Within a year, my mother died suddenly of a heart attack. The news crushed me, especially after everything else. I loved and deeply admired my mother, for her gentleness, her humility, and her unselfish service to others, but she died so unexpectedly I never had the chance to tell her, or to say goodbye. My father was also unwell, so I moved back home to Syria to care for him, a normal practice even today in the Middle East. I took baby Leila with me.

Being my father's caregiver was a labor of love, and reminded me of what love meant, what a well-lived life looked like. When he died, the entire city of Damascus seemed to show up for his funeral. He was a humble shopkeeper by trade, but everyone knew they could trust him, that they could count on him, no matter what. His employees were grief stricken, as he often sacrificed his own profit for their well-being. Hundreds of people poured out countless stories of his generosity and kindness. I never knew.

One powerful, quiet way he served was by acting as an "unofficial banker." In Syria at the time, the concept of banks was still new and many people didn't trust them with their money. After my father died, we opened the big safe in his store, astonished to find the equivalent of hundreds of thousands of dollars. Each bundle was neatly tied and stacked, with a note attached identifying whose money it was, and the date they'd given it to my father. Hundreds of people had trusted my father with their life savings! We returned all the bundles to their rightful owners, and I learned by my father's example how to serve God by serving others.

My father's life inspired me, and I realized that was who I wanted to be—a humble, trustworthy servant.

This inspiration and all of my recent losses gave me the courage to face my biggest challenge—my marriage. Once again, I asked for a divorce, and once again my husband pleaded with me to try again, making promises to mend his ways. For a short time I moved back, but it wasn't long before he relapsed. How could he not, without the help he needed? Eyes open, heart certain, I proceeded with divorce.

Not surprisingly, given Muslim society at the time and his family's financial situation, my husband got full custody of the children, even though he traveled frequently. He retained all of our assets. I left Dubai alone, penniless and grief-stricken, but there was nothing I could do, at least for the moment. I moved to Syria to live with my sister and her family, which wasn't easy, especially given the privileged life I'd recently led.

I needed to support myself financially, and I took up sewing. Assisting my mother as a child, I had learned the essentials of the craft, and had picked up some of her talent and creativity for designing beautiful and unique designs for women. I knew I had to get back on my feet, to get Leila back in my life and to win visitation rights with my sons.

My brother, who lived in the US, had a brain tumor and needed surgery, so I traveled to be with him and help care for him. He recovered, and I took the opportunity to visit family in the States. I met a third cousin in Michigan, and, with the blessing and approval of my family, I married him. You would think I would move more cautiously, after my first marriage, but God smiled on us, and we have been happy for many years.

My new husband had three young children; I, of course, had two sons in English boarding school and Leila, who was then six and living in Dubai with her father. My husband's kids were thoroughly 'westernized', something very difficult for me to accept at first. I had traditional Muslim expectations, including modest dress, disciplined conduct, respectful language, and daily chores and studies. I struggled to be a kind and loving mother to my new stepchildren, learning to accept some of their western ways. I look back now and I can laugh. But then, I was not laughing. I was praying hard for the patience and perspective to be a good mother!

Once we had settled into our new family life, I begged my first husband to let Leila come live with us and, to my relief and joy, he agreed. I threw myself into caring for this new, integrated family, and building a career. I continued with sewing and studied fashion design, and launched a small but successful business designing and manufacturing elegant women's clothing.

It was also around this time that I would say I developed a more mature spiritual life. I found comfort and strength in the religious rituals of my childhood and turned back to them in a way I hadn't through my adult life. Perhaps it was my newfound contentment, or the many trials I'd endured, or some combination of them, but I took to expressing thanks and gratitude to the God of my childhood in traditional ways. I was happy, prosperous, safe; I had the love of a good man and children who adored me. Things rolled along smoothly.

And then, they didn't.

My husband was laid off from the job he loved. Unable to find anything that interested him, he invested in a prosperous area gas station and opened an auto shop. But the franchise owner consolidated and forced him to close the gas station, without compensation. The auto shop failed. We fell into bankruptcy; my husband fell into depression.

Meanwhile, I was trying to keep the family together, fed, and in good spirits, while also trying to grow my business and earn enough money for us to survive. It wasn't working. Perhaps my lowest moment was when I crossed the threshold of the welfare office to apply for food stamps. I knew I couldn't do it, it wasn't the right thing for us, and I prayed to God for guidance. It came, and I broke down and called my wealthy brother in Syria for help. He was shocked and hurt that I hadn't let him know earlier how dire our circumstances were, but I'd been ashamed at what I considered our failure.

He reminded me, in words and deeds, that families were there for each other. Another lesson in love and humility. Surely, then, this was the answer to our prayers?

He helped us while I threw myself into expanding my clothing business. It grew rapidly and I was sure God was smiling on us. I decided to move from a small warehouse to a much larger one, but while I was negotiating a new lease, I let my business insurance lapse. A very costly mistake. Incredibly, a fire swept though the small warehouse and I lost all of my work, fabric, designs, and inventory. Everything that I had worked so hard to create, up in smoke!

I was devastated and exhausted, and once again found myself in tears. But my precious Leila served as God's wake-up call. She said to me, "Mommy, I'm so sorry that you lost your business. I know that you worked really hard to build it and that you were proud of your success. But now that it is gone, you will have more time to be with me!"

Her innocent words, spoken to console me, hit hard. In my fervor to build my business, when I was with my children, I wasn't really present. I had sacrificed their needs for the demands of my thriving business. I firmly resolved not to rebuild, but to focus on my children, and to become more involved in my community. It was a painful, but necessary message. Sometimes an apparent loss carries with it the seed of blessings that are so much richer! God was urging me to spend more time with my children, and the fire was His way of getting my attention.

My husband eventually found work again, in the field he loves. We are not wealthy, but we are content. Life's trials have schooled me in ways that I could not have imagined as a little girl growing up in a loving, sheltered home in Syria or as a hopeful, jet-setting newly-wed in Dubai.

I have learned the meaning of life. This lifetime is short, compared to the hereafter. When you're happy or comfortable in your ways, it's easy to get neglectful of God. You stop listening for His voice in your life. Struggle, pain, setbacks, and loss can lead to spiritual maturity. It's not a pretty picture sometimes. We all have a choice in enduring a painful loss—to turn toward God for comfort, strength, and understanding or to turn away from God in bitterness and despair.

When we choose bitterness, we conclude that our prayers

have not been answered. But this is not so. When our prayers seem to go unanswered, I believe that it is because we're not ready to receive God's answer. We're not spiritually mature enough to hear the answer. We're not patient. We want what we want, and we want it right now! It may take an entire lifetime to understand God's plan, or even beyond. God's plan is eternal. So when you are in darkness, doubt, despair, pain and suffering, turn TOWARD God, not away from Him.

I want to share the following story to illustrate my point:

Back in Syria, a friend of our family, a well-educated man, had three beautiful daughters. His daughters were intellectually gifted, and after excelling in high school, all three went on to earn advanced degrees at top western universities in medicine and science. The father was very proud, and felt sure that God had rewarded him for his discipline and devotion in raising such talented and gifted young women.

When his wife became pregnant with their fourth child, a son, he was delighted! But the son was born with Down's syndrome and the father was aghast. Rather than accepting and loving his son, he railed against God for delivering this cruel mistake. The child's very presence was a constant reminder of how God had inflicted his family with hardship.

The father worked hard to home school his son. He sought European doctors for a cure, but in spite of his best efforts, his son remained severely limited in his mental abilities. When his daughters left for college, the son remained. The parents grew older and their health declined. When the mother grew truly ill, the son, now big and strong, was the only one who could lift her, to bathe, dress and care for her. He fussed over her tenderly, tirelessly attending to all of the repetitive tasks required in caring for a bed-ridden patient. The father experienced a change of heart. He realized that after all the years of cursing God for His 'mistake of a son,' this boy had been sent to care for them in their old age. The mother died, and the boy took care of his father, too. Before he died, the father confessed to his son how he had considered him a 'mistake'. He begged his forgiveness. The son didn't understand, and shrugged it off. He just did what he loved doing—taking care of his parents, which he did until both were gone. Within months of his parents' deaths, the son died as well, having far outlived the normal life expectancy of a person with Down's syndrome. The three daughters, all with thriving professions and families of their own, understood God's lesson. God's plan may not appear to look like a plan at all—more like a mistake sometimes. Each of the daughters returned as disciplined practitioners of their Muslim faith, their eyes opened to God's love through their brother's example.

So, I guess my final thoughts are that it doesn't matter so much how often you pray, or how closely you read your scriptures and understand your theology. I have said the same morning prayers for decades now. The prayers remain unchanged—I am the one who has changed. If these blessed rituals are not joined with a conscious choice to serve God's creatures, then they become almost devoid of their true meaning. To me, what matters most is that you serve others in their time of need. The gift of having endured great suffering is the ability to understand and demonstrate great compassion. Suffering that is shared is lightened. I am a better listener and companion now. I know how to stay present with, to simply be with, people who are suffering. God makes it easy for me to show up, listen with compassion, and help others.

I am fond of saying, show me a captain with many battle scars and wounds, and I'll show you a great captain! My scars remind me of the battles I have faced. God has purified me in

the intense heat of struggle, and has shown me mercy and
compassion without measure. It is up to me to show that same
mercy and compassion to others in need. I may never completely know or understand God's plan for my life, but I completely trust His wisdom and that whatever His plan, it's better than mine.

Looking back over the years I realize that God had a plan
for me, even when I didn't understand it. I wish that I had
stayed close to God throughout my entire life. I missed out on
so much because I was spiritually immature. I am thankful
that I understand now, that spiritual maturity comes through
a lifetime of tribulations, and discipline through prayer, devotion, scripture reading, fasting and acts of charity. I had to
be brought to my knees by circumstances, too many and too
painful to face alone, before I understood what I was missing.
It all started with losing my son, Marwan. That was my turning point in returning to God.

Today, service and interconnectedness are two major
themes for me. I am a devout, practicing Muslim, active in
interfaith projects in my community. I pray five times daily. I
fast on Holy days. I join small groups studying the Q'uran, as
well as the life and words of the Prophet Muhammed, what
we call hadith. I am an active volunteer, frequently invited to
speak publicly at community and interfaith events. My parents taught me well, and today I show up when someone needs
help. It doesn't matter who they are, or what faith they follow.
This is the work that God calls me to do and I do it joyfully.

This is my favorite prayer from the opening of the Q'uran, called Al-Fatiha. I repeat it at least 17 times a day:

In the name of God, the Most Gracious, the Most Merciful:

Praise be to God, the Lord of the Universe.

The Most Gracious, the Most Merciful.

King of the Day of Judgment.

You alone we worship, and You alone we ask for help.

Guide us to the straight way;

The way of those whom you have blessed, not of those who have deserved anger, nor of those who stray.

Amin (Amen).

CHAPTER FIVE

Brenda

Faith, gratitude and forgiveness—three cornerstones of a spiritual life, we're told. But few of us are ever called upon to walk through fire to reflect them. Spiritual challenges, the big ones, make us question what we believe and how we will face life in the aftermath. For those lucky enough to know Brenda, they have a true-life role model of faith in action, a friend who has retained grace through tragedy and loss.

Brenda wasn't sure how she was going to manage life after divorce, with three young children in tow. Her marriage had taken her to Georgia, far away from her large family and her Utah hometown, where she'd been born and raised in the Church of Jesus Christ of Latter Day Saints (LDS). As a single mother, she focused on keeping her children healthy and in good spirits after her husband left.

All this changed one day when she met another single parent in a classroom. Joe Crummy was a consummate southern gentlemen, kind, respectful, quick to praise, slow to anger, and a devoted father to his daughter. He completely defied his last name, despite Brenda's playful teasing. He owned a stone and stucco business and soon stole her heart. It was a simple, sweet courtship; they married a year later.

Though raised Catholic, Joe studied the LDS faith during their courtship and surprised Brenda when he converted before their wedding. Despite his successful business, Joe and Brenda left Georgia behind for Utah, to establish roots in Brenda's hometown, surrounded by her parents and eight brothers and sisters. He would have to start his business from scratch, but he believed family came first and knew they would all benefit surrounded by a large, loving, close-knit family.

Brenda and Joe couldn't have been happier. Joe set up business in Utah as a contractor, overseeing building sites and construction. The work was hard and financially straining, as all new businesses are, but life in Utah was perfect for them. Newlywed happy and settling into a satisfying family routine, Joe proved himself even more as a humble, easygoing, capable man, handling the stress of the move and the complete overhaul of his life with calm affability.

They practiced their faith daily in family prayer and scripture reading. They attended church services weekly, immersing themselves in their new community, aware of the rich blessings of their new life. Soon after the move, Brenda discovered she was pregnant—one of the greatest blessings yet. Joe was thrilled! He made plans to set up the bassinet on his side of the bed, so he could wake up first and bring the baby to Brenda. They chose a name for the baby boy—Trevor Joe. Everything had fallen into place.

January 9, 2004 changed everything.

Brenda, nine months pregnant and still wrapped in a towel from her mid-morning shower, answered the knock on the door to find a uniformed officer on her doorstep. Her heart dropped. She knew something was dreadfully wrong, a feeling that grew only worse when he asked if he could come in and sit down with her. She held her breath and pulled at the collar of her robe, feeling vulnerable and exposed. Nothing could have prepared her for the awful truth.

Joe had been murdered that morning, shot multiple times in the head, neck and shoulders, sitting in his truck at one of his worksites.

Brenda couldn't believe it. She could barely breathe. She grabbed the officer's arm and sank to the ground. She asked him to sit with her for a while since she was home alone. The well-intentioned officer tried to console her. "We think we have the guy who killed him."

To this day Brenda vividly remembers her reaction. How could that possibly help? It didn't bring her husband, her beloved Joe, the father of her unborn child, back.

Time stood still. She squeezed the officer's hand for a long time, sobbing, hoping and praying Joe didn't suffer or linger long. The dream was over. Their new son, Trevor, was due in less than two weeks. Now he would never know his daddy who'd been so excited for him to get here.

Brenda, shocked, numb and barely functioning, had to prepare for a funeral and a birth. The story made headline news, and friends and family stepped in, "circling the wagons" to protect Brenda and her children from the media storm while they absorbed the horrifying truth. Brenda's family made the necessary funeral arrangements, sparing her from the excruciating task. Meals were brought in, neighbors tended the kids. Joe's body wasn't released for days after the murder, until the police had concluded their investigation. The first time Brenda saw him again was at the viewing, just prior to the funeral. She broke down sobbing.

Within days of the funeral, Brenda went into labor. Again, her family circled around her, maintaining a protective vigil at the hospital, freeing her from drop-in visitors or explanations to the staff about the missing father. Trevor Joe's birth was bittersweet. Trevor was a living testimony to her loving marriage, and a painful reminder that Joe wasn't there to share the birth of the baby he'd so anticipated. Brenda worried about his future, all of their futures. How could she be mommy and daddy to four children with no money, no income and a newborn? She knew she'd have to find a way.

The mission of surviving day-to-day began in earnest as soon as she got home from the hospital. She prayed desperately for the strength to carry on, silently and aloud with her children. In her prayers, she asked Joe to watch over them and help her. She gratefully accepted help from family and friends. Meals poured in. Groceries "appeared" in her refrigerator. Offers to baby sit were frequent. Her brother took on the task of shutting down Joe's business—a complex undertaking of paying contractors and suppliers, collecting money owed and liquidating thousands of pieces of equipment.

Then there was the overwhelming business of dealing with the actual crime.

Joe's murderer was an illegal immigrant from Mexico working for his father, a legal subcontractor at Joe's site. As is often the case in construction, Joe was waiting for the builder to make a payment before he paid the subcontractors. The man was angry and wanted his money, but his father wouldn't pay him until he received money from Joe. Joe had spoken to him a few times, reassuring him that his father would be paid as soon as he was, and then he could take up what he was owed with his father. But his answers did not satisfy the man, so instead, he seethed, waiting gun-in-hand for Joe to arrive that fateful morning at the work site, gunning him down in plain view of a string of witnesses.

It all seemed completely senseless to Brenda. The man who murdered Joe over a few hundred dollars was an illegal immigrant with a felony record for smuggling other illegal immigrants and possession of firearms. He was also a husband and father of three children.

After some legal wrangling, the man pled guilty. Brenda saw him for the first time at his sentencing hearing, when the judge asked her to describe the impact the crime had on her and her children. Calmly and clearly, Brenda spoke her truth, free of self-pity or over-dramatization. Brenda simply described what it was like to be widowed at age 35 with a newborn, 3 small children, no husband and no household income.

She was acutely aware of the fact that the man's outrageous act had left both their families struggling, fatherless and bereft.

Brenda spoke to the man directly. She looked him straight in the eye and said, clearly and slowly, "I forgive you. I will never forget what you've done and I forgive you."

His sentence was twenty years to life.

When discussing what it means to forgive, Brenda explains that it's essential to forgive others, especially one's enemies. "Jesus taught us this and I was brought up with this lesson my whole life, in my faith and in my family. Forgiving Joe's murderer puts the principle of forgiveness into action. I wanted to teach my children, by example, to forgive others." She harbors no hint of revenge, animosity or bitterness toward the man. "It's just not in my makeup to hate someone. I don't want my children growing up hating anyone. It's my job to teach them to love others, no matter what. We can hate what they do, but we must learn to love everyone, unconditionally. It's what our Savior taught us, it's what I will do as best I can."

She is particularly sensitive to this in terms of her children's reaction to the man's race. Because he was Mexican, the children began to fear Latino men. Brenda noticed her children cowering when they saw them and moving perceptibly away from them if they were nearby. As an extension of the lesson of forgiveness, she works with them to overcome this fear, to remember to love people as children of God, not to judge them by their physical appearance, race, language, or culture. Yes, a man who murdered their dad happened to be Mexican, but that was a consequence of the choices he made as an individual, not a reflection of his race. She wants her children to grow up free from fear, prejudice or hatred of any person, but especially as a reaction to race, nationality or skin color.

Today, Brenda continues to raise four children alone. She works part-time as a dental receptionist, but her small paycheck barely covers the essentials. Financial stress is a way of life, as is worry over the lack of a father figure in her children's lives. And yet, she copes.

For one thing, Brenda focuses on what is good in her life—her children, her health, her family and friends and her faith. She prays daily and teaches her children to do the same. "I try not to think too far into the future. If I did, I think I would fall into deep depression. I have no idea how I'm going to provide for this family and be a good mom. Because we were working so hard to set up the business here, we never got around to buying life insurance. I know that causes Joe great pain too, wherever he is. We had talked about it; we just hadn't done it yet. Financial insecurity is my greatest worry. I am willing to do my part, but I am turning the details over to God. I don't know what the future holds. I stay focused on today, and what is good."

Joe's memory and legacy of love is palpable in their home,

aided by Trevor, a cheerful, energetic toddler who looks just like his Dad. In playful moments, Brenda reminds him laughingly, "Trevor, it's up to you to keep the Crummy name alive!" Joe's clothes still hang in their bedroom closet. The children wear his shirts to bed. They talk often, pray often and share fond stories and memories of Joe, which helps them remember and cherish him, focusing on his life and his love, not his murder.

Nighttime is the hardest part of the day for Brenda. She reads and prays with her children, tucks them into bed, then hopes for a quick, deep sleep. Brenda feels Joe's presence most closely at church and when she runs or plays tennis. These places and activities clear her head, and she feels "light" again.

Her faith and courage sustain her, and sometimes, she believes, offer her their own gifts. Two years after Joe's death, Brenda found a slip of paper in her scriptures. Opening it, she discovered an essay, "The Ten Things I Love Most about Brenda," Joe's homework assignment from a premarital class. It moved Brenda to tears both joyful, for having loved and married Joe, and sorrowful, for having lost him so soon. "I would never wish this experience on anyone, and, in some respects, I will always be in recovery from losing Joe. I am lucky in that I am not prone to depression. I feel truly blessed for my great family and friends. They are gifts and they make sure that I am showered with kindness and caring. I feel stronger too—spiritually, physically and emotionally. I am never alone, even though I am on my own as a single mom with four kids. God works through other people. They just 'show up' and bring me hope, a meal, help with the kids, a job referral, a good laugh."

Despite all she's endured, Brenda still manages to be grateful, live her faith, and find strength and courage in forgiveness. Her warm generous smiles, willingness to enjoy a good belly laugh, and frequent spontaneous expressions of gratitude reflect her determination to live a joyful life and make sure her children know a fun, vibrant woman rather than a grieving widow who's withdrawn from life.

While she turned to others to help her survive tragic circumstances, she has become a true inspiration to those around her. In the face of such loss and devastating circumstances, Brenda is fiercely determined to continue counting her blessings. Humbled by such grace, we are reminded to count our own.

CHAPTER SIX

Jean

When I think about it, so much of my spiritual journey revolves around experiences of death. Perhaps that's one reason I wound up a Tibetan Buddhist, a spiritual tradition that focuses on death as just another cycle of life, rather than the end of it. This ancient religion gave us the Tibetan Book of the Dead, even today considered a watershed text for preparing both the dying and their survivors for the event, and its aftermath.

I was raised in Illinois, a practicing Methodist in a large family, one sister and four brothers. My mother was active in the church, my father less so, until the shattering loss of my five-year-old brother Shorty when I was nine. And I should say, we didn't simply lose him. He drowned in the lake in front of our house, and we searched for him for hours before we found his body. It was awful.

It was especially difficult since the year before, my mother suffered a stillbirth after a full-term pregnancy. The combination of those tragic events was very hard on us, and we never really dealt with our grief as a family. We never talked about it, or shared our feelings with each other. We just struggled on quietly, each of us in our own way.

Church wasn't exactly a refuge, either. When the minister told my mother that she should be happy for Shorty, because he was with God, she was angry and hurt and found a different place to worship. We kids were involved in the first church in a social way, so we stayed there, active in the choir and youth activities. My dad, "Pop," dropped out altogether. I can't say it was a spiritual time for us, especially not for me, and especially not in a church setting.

Around that time I remember reading the Bible, a contemporary version. I think I was ten. Lying in bed, I would read and have long "conversations" with God and Jesus. I found solace in my private prayers and reading. Even then, I derived more benefit from personal spiritual practice than from communal worship, something that has stayed with me to this day. During high school, I drifted more and more away from church, until I hardly had any relationship with it at all.

Years later, I fell in love with my now-husband Jerry, a devout Buddhist. When we were dating, I made a point of avoiding Buddhism because I didn't want to convert to a religion *because* of a man.

Nonetheless, when his father was dying and Jerry went to be with him in Oklahoma, I agreed to do a simple mantra, a mantra which any Tibetan Buddhist child would know, "Om mani padme hung." I opened myself up to a deity of compassion and requested that same compassion surround his dying father. Lighting a candle, I repeated the mantra thousands of times, in some small way supporting Jerry and his father during this intense time, connecting to them from miles away.

And within, I felt a different connection.

After his father died and Jerry returned, I continued this

simple mantra practice for years. In 1991, Jerry and I traveled to Nepal together and I met his teacher, a simple, profound practitioner of the Tibetan Buddhist tradition, Tulku Urgyen Rinpoche.

In Nepal, I made two big life decisions: I accepted Tibetan Buddhism as my spiritual path and I married Jerry.

Today Jerry and I and our ten-year old daughter, Abriel, live in Salt Lake City. A teacher, I continue my daily practices, integrating Buddhist philosophy into my daily life. There are two main teachings in Buddhism. First, everything, everyone is impermanent. Not one single thing fails to change with time—not nations, not mountains, not buildings, not relationships, not people. Nothing has permanency. We deeply contemplate impermanence and death, not just intellectually, but experientially through daily repetitive chanting, mantras and silent meditation. By slowing down, we notice when we are clinging to or craving pleasure, or avoiding or pushing away pain. It is the craving or averting that causes suffering, not a person or event itself.

Second, everything and everyone is interdependent. Nothing, no one is alone. When a rock is thrown into a pond, water ripples from the point of entry, affecting the pool well beyond where it hits. Every action, every word has a consequence. As humans, we are largely unconscious of this idea, and of the consequences we set in motion by our actions. Buddhists believe we must train ourselves to be mindful; we cultivate awareness through our daily practice of prayer and meditation.

Contemplating death is huge, the ultimate demonstration of the impermanence of life. We know this intellectually, but we don't take it to heart until there's a sudden accident or diagnosis, or something traumatic, and then we recoil in shock and disbelief. Really, if we're true to our religious beliefs, we should be shocked when it *doesn't* happen. We should be surprised and delighted when we wake up any given morning, and notice in the awakening conscious mind, "Oh wow, I'm still here, still alive, and most of my parts seem to be working!"

Of course, like any religious conviction, it remains a mere belief, an abstract concept until reality puts you and your ideals to the test. When I lost my brother and my father to cancer within two months of each other, it was time to live my values. And I am blessed to say that not only did they get me through this emotional, painful ordeal, I believe they made a difference in how my traumatized family experienced these events, tempered to some extent with love, acceptance and peace.

In March 2006, Pop was diagnosed with cancer of the spine. We were hopeful at first. It was treatable, and he went into radiation treatment. But then it moved into his lungs. There was nothing more medicine could do for him. They sent him home, with the advice to maintain as high a quality of life as he could, for as long he could.

Still processing my dad's prognosis, letting it settle into my mind and heart, I was devastated when my mother called to tell me that on top of it, my fifty-three year old brother, Mark, had a rare, aggressive form of tongue cancer. We were baffled. Mark never smoked or chewed tobacco. He took good care of himself. A gentle, kind, open-hearted man, a loving father of three children and the "fun uncle" to his nieces and nephews, we couldn't believe he was dying.

Reeling from the news, I called Mark immediately. I'll never forget what he said to me. "My goal is to outlive both Mom and Pop because they shouldn't have to face another child's death." Just like Mark, always thinking of others.

Mark is my hero. He began to physically decline in October and endured so much pain until he died the following March. Tumors rose up and broke open around his neck. He couldn't swallow, and required a feeding tube in the final few months. His three kids, ages 24, 19, and 15 were amazing and took such good care of him at home, while still keeping up with their busy schedules at school and work.

My family pitched in as much as possible. One of my brothers took Mark to doctor appointments and helped him make decisions about his cancer treatment while my mom and dad helped out when they could. Still, by early January, Mark felt that his care was becoming unduly stressful for his kids, so Mom asked him to move in with her and Dad, a few miles away. By that time, neither Dad nor Mark had any real chance of a cure, and treatment at that point meant palliative care. My dad was on oxygen, but could still get up, visit friends and go out. Mark was confined to a bed.

It was a strange time. Mark and Pop were very close, but even so, I remember thinking how surreal the situation was, when in effect, my brother had moved back into my father's house to die with him. In some ways, it was lovely they could be together, beautiful for them to have each other. And of course, it was stressful, too, especially on my mom. A hospice nurse visited once a week to treat them both, but for the most part the care giving fell to my mother, though the rest of the family rallied around as best they could.

Mark's kids visited daily. My final brother moved in from Florida for the last few months. My brother in the area stopped in daily as well, and my sister, who lived an hour away, came on week-ends. I lived thousands of miles away, but I would visit as I could, sometimes with Abriel. While I was there I would organize the calendar and shift schedules so that Dad,

Mark and Mom had people with them all the time as much as possible.

Somehow, my Buddhism had made an impression on my family. Mom told me she'd seen change in me since I began my Buddhist practice, that I'd become more peaceful, more accepting, and calmer. Facing Mark's imminent death, she became adamant that I be there when it happened. I don't know where my mother's faith in me came from, but she was convinced I would help Mark, that I could guide him through a peaceful death process. I had no direct experience, but my years of Buddhist practice, cultivating mindfulness, loving kindness and acceptance, was being called into action.

My visits became part of my spiritual journey, especially in conversations with Mark. For the first time ever, we talked at length about Shorty, about the impact of his death on our family and our spirituality. Mark believed in a God, because he didn't know how else we could explain all the big questions —life, nature, and the universe. He didn't actively participate in a church, but he was open to different spiritual insights and interpretations, especially as he neared death.

My husband Jerry always sent a gift for Mark with me when I traveled, and one of these was a Buddhist pendant with a blessing cord—a knot tied for each of the blessings prayed for that person. After I explained what it meant, Mark held it close, determined to keep it with him as he lay in bed. He kept it close through the final weeks of his life.

Mark asked me for guidance in dying, looking for a peaceful journey. Sometimes I would look at him and ask, "Mark, are you dying right now, in this moment?" And he would smile and say, "No, not in this moment; in this moment, I'm still here!"

Then he would contemplate his situation. "I've had a good

life. I wouldn't mind a few more years, but I'm OK with things as they are. I hate leaving my kids so soon, and I feel sorry for Mom and Pop, knowing they'll go through the loss of another son. But all in all, I am fine with my life. I have no regrets about anything."

He took a thorough inventory of each person he was close to. "Do you think they're ready for me to die? How can we help him (or her) prepare for me to die?" That was Mark in a nutshell. Even in his own death, he wanted to serve the people he loved. He was so other-centered that way. He'd even been a hospice volunteer before he became sick, one of those rare individuals who just "gets it," that we're here for only a temporary visit, and we don't get to choose the timing or circumstances of our departure.

He didn't like receiving so much attention. I reassured him that this was our opportunity to serve him and generate positive merit, an important Buddhism principle. We also discussed reincarnation, a Buddhist belief. Mark was genuinely curious, so I explained that energy, the essence of who we are, has to go somewhere when we die, and that we believe that when physical death of the body occurs, its energy takes form in another body for another life.

We return as sentient beings with a consciousness, over and over again, until we achieve a state of enlightenment. Tibetan Buddhists also take a vow to continue to reincarnate even after enlightenment to be of service until all suffering is relieved from all beings. The Dalai Lama is recognized as a manifestation of such a being who has reincarnated to help those who suffer. I like to use the analogy of a candle. The candle is lit, and from that light, the energy is transferred to another candle by lighting it from the same flame. The original candle eventually expires, but the energy is transferred.

The "self contained identity" called Mark does not transfer to the next life, but his energy or essence does. I don't think Mark was completely convinced about reincarnation, but the explanation seemed to comfort him.

A few days before Mark died, Pop was next to his bed holding his hand. Mark experienced about twenty pain-free minutes, and a feeling of wide open spaciousness and light. My dad sensed it too, but they didn't talk about then. When Mark told me about it, he said, "I felt like I could have let go into it."

"The next time that happens, just do it, let go into it, Mark," I urged him. In Buddhism, we believe that all beings have a primordial, enlightened mind, free from concepts. Mark called it "the God mind." During life, in your body, you catch glimpses of this natural mind. Buddha means enlightened being...there are many. The historical Buddha happens to be the one who originally taught and transmitted the teachings. Highly realized, or highly enlightened, means that we are able to operate out of our primordial mind more of the time. If you recognize this open spaciousness through meditation and mantra practice, then you can let go into it. If you don't understand or practice being in this state, then it can scare you and you start grasping or craving, shutting off the natural mind.

The Tibetan Book of the Dead offers specific training on what to do at the time of death, how to let go of craving, attachment, and the desire for things to be other than they are—all of which lead to suffering—and to recognize one's own innate enlightened quality. The key is to open to your spacious self during your lifetime in the ordinary moments, and not wait until you're on your deathbed to try to learn this. I shared all of these things with Mark, not with the purpose of converting him to a religion, but to help him find a peaceful way to be with his own death process.

In early March, I left my mother's house on a Tuesday, after telling Mark how much I appreciated him, how proud I was of him—his integrity, his sense of humor, his unselfishness and his ability to find meaning in life until the very end. I promised him I would do everything I could to be there when he died.

By Friday, he started slipping in and out of consciousness so I flew back as soon as I could. I arrived about midnight on Saturday and sat with him the rest of the night. He wasn't responding, but his breathing was peaceful and I believe that he could hear and sense me. I recited mantras, and sang and talked to him. "You're dying now, relax into it, you can do this," I reassured him.

Early morning, my mom and a brother relieved me so I could sleep. I whispered in Mark's ear, "If you're going to die, today is an excellent day. Your whole family will be here...it's Sunday." Everyone gathered at my parents' home. Just after 11 am, Mark's breathing changed and my mom called us into his room. "Let go Mark, we're all here. Let go, relax into death," I said to him. My words were very direct and personal, and I was worried I would upset my family, but my mom urged me to go on. We surrounded him, touching and talking to him. He took one long last breath in, and let it out slowly. Then he died.

It may sound odd, but it was a beautiful death, a peaceful, complete death. My mom pinned the Buddha pendant on him and we kept his body for hours before calling the mortuary. We hung out at the house together, drank tea, ate lunch and visited with his body. His kids listened to music, selecting something just right for his funeral. We all agreed we wanted to die the way that Mark had. Maybe that's why he died first, at a relatively young age. He showed us all how to die.

According to the steps laid out in the Tibetan Book of the Dead, I spent forty-nine days saying specific prayers and mantras for my brother, and offered little acts of service to him and my family. These are meant to guide the transitional passage of the soul, but they may also be designed to keep those left behind busy, offering them a way to continue in service to the dead, rather than slipping into restless, purposeless mourning. To put it simply, these rituals helped me help my brother and family, and they comforted me.

We laid Mark's ashes to rest at the foot of Shorty's grave, with a small headstone that read, "Mark and Shorty, brothers."

After Mark's funeral, my mom and dad needed some time alone. We didn't know how much longer Pop would survive, and we all needed time to regroup. When dad told me how beautiful he thought Mark's death was, I promised him we would do everything possible to offer him the same peaceful, comforting presence through his death. Witnessing Mark's passing comforted him and gave him much needed courage to face his own death.

Dad was a philosopher and a businessman; he had a sense of a Higher Power, but not one that he would call God. He was a calm, quiet, easy-going person and he set everything in place before he died. He stopped going out in early April. He was pretty matter of fact about things. He sorted through his clothing with my sister. "I'm not sure about whether I'll be wearing those summer clothes, but for sure I won't need my winter clothes," he remarked. He had taken precise care of his and my mom's finances, had all of the key papers in order, and had even finished that year's tax return well ahead of schedule.

He was bedridden for less than a week. With lung cancer,

we knew that he could easily die in his sleep. I wanted to keep my promise and be there for him, so Abriel and I flew out when he took to his bed. My two remaining brothers and sister arrived. We stayed with him round the clock for that week. Sometimes, Pop's breathing changed and we would all sit by his side. He would struggle, then regain a calmer breathing pattern. We slept on the floor next to him. It was nice to be together as a family, in this sacred journey. Mentally, Pop had been emotionally ready to die the week before. The cancer was invading his brain; he was getting confused, and he didn't want to die that way.

Of course, Mom was a great concern for Dad. In Buddhism, we believe that we are not to cling to a dying person by crying in their presence, a concept that has become more common, even in Western hospice care. The idea is that there will be plenty of opportunity to mourn after they are gone. While someone is still alive, it should be our goal to make the dying process supportive and peaceful; to allow the person the dignity to die their own way, in their own time.

Mom deeply understood this and spent many quiet hours alone with Pop in their last few days together. Still, it was a hard time for her, and one day, when Dad's blood pressure plummeted, she started to cry.

Worried, he asked us, "Is she going to be okay?"

It was our opportunity to comfort him, to let him know we would take care of Mom, and that he was free to go when he decided the time was right.

Dad died early Friday morning, before the sun rose. My brother and I, sleeping next to him, heard his breathing change. We woke everyone up to gather around him. "Okay, Pop, it's time. Just let go," I encouraged him. His breathing wasn't as peaceful as Mark's had been because of the lung cancer. Dying was hard work for him and he had to be patient. Emotionally ready, he had to allow his body to shut down. Both Mark and Pop died the way they wanted to, on beautiful, peaceful spring mornings, with birds singing and morning light bathing the room. Mom climbed into bed next to him, to hold him one last time.

Again, we kept the body for several hours, and we buried my father's ashes with Mark and Shorty.

I like to think I've faced these deaths with grace and courage; that my Buddhist practices and beliefs offered my father and my brother peaceful loving journeys into death. I am still grieving them, of course, and the effect their deaths had on my family. My Buddhist friends tell me, "Jean, we're really sorry for your loss. But you know you're Buddhist, that's just the way things are." This might strike some people as cold, but I smile when they say it. I get it. People die. Animals die. It is helpful to remember that there are no exceptions. It's a reality. I don't wrestle with "why" or "why me?" It's our nature, nothing's permanent.

That's not to say we don't have feelings. A Buddhist has the same intensity of emotions and thoughts as everyone else. I just accept it, all of it. I cry. Sometimes I sob. I feel the pain and longing. I let it out, I don't hold back or judge myself as "less Buddhist like" for feeling great sadness. *I don't let my mind tell my heart how to interpret the pain.* Sometimes I feel like an observer of my own process. The pain, the sadness, the up and down of the emotional roller coaster—it's all part of loving deeply and letting go.

Allow yourself to have strong emotions. Be with them, learn from them, and befriend them. Don't push your feelings away, but also, don't cling to them. Be willing to look at them and recognize patterns. Strong emotions dissolve on their own when they aren't attached to our perceptions of what is fair or unfair. We feel them, and then let them go. If they linger, and we dwell on them, then we allow them to attach to a story. The strong emotions are then our thoughts about our sadness, our clinging to who used to be here and how it was when he or she was here. It's our aversion to what we don't want, and our craving of what we do want—this is the source of our suffering. It's all part of learning to let go and to let life happen, on life's terms.

Allow yourself to ask questions about your own spiritual beliefs, and let others ask them. My daughter Abriel keeps asking what happens after this life. She tells me it's all just beliefs, and she wants to know how we really know. I don't know how to answer her. Yes, it is all just beliefs; we cannot prove anything. Nobody can. You have to decide for yourself what you believe. You have to decide what kind of person you will be, today, in this moment. And you have to choose what beliefs will support you best in being that kind of person.

She's not satisfied with my answer. She reminds me of myself at that age. Always wondering, always questioning. I encourage her to explore the question for herself. I don't try to convince her or convert her. She'll find her own answers, in her own time.

I actually had a dream about Mark recently. I asked him Abriel's question, what really happens after you die? He told me that his body slowly dissolved, and he shed his clothes because he didn't need them any more. After that, he was met by a monk, who guided him to the next stage of life. I got the sense Mark was on a journey, which makes perfect sense to me.

Once, in tears, Mom asked me, "What are we supposed to learn from all of this?" I understand her distress, but I encouraged her to not think of it as a "supposed to learn" event, as if somehow it's a great big test, but rather to ask herself "what *can* I learn, or what *am* I learning from this?" It's so much more empowering and helpful to frame it that way, at least for me.

If I were to offer advice to those inclined to listen, I would urge them to fully embrace and practice whatever spiritual path they are on as a means of living everyday life—whatever it may bring. For me it was taking up a daily meditation and mantra practice of letting go. Especially after the stress of losing Mark and my father, if I'm not disciplined in following my daily rituals, I am more emotional and vulnerable, less available to others; I'm much more likely to 'react' than 'respond' to people and situations.

Through regular practice, a commitment to centering your mind and heart, no matter what the spiritual tradition, one can learn to let go of the small everyday stuff that we all wrestle with, especially our own inner chatter—you know, the reactive thoughts and emotions that swirl within. Then when the big stuff hits, and it will, we won't be an unconscious slave to our reactions. "Letting go" will naturally kick in. Practice in letting go of the small stuff, enables you to let go of the big stuff when the time comes.

CHAPTER SEVEN

Marsha

Tempering is a heat treatment technique used to strengthen steel, making it more flexible and less brittle. Comparisons are often made in spiritual circles, when a person withstands one trial after another, changing in the journey to a stronger, more supple being.

For Marsha, a retired social worker and probations officer who had spent her career working with troubled youth, the journey to a new spiritual consciousness began the day her older sister, ArLee, suffered severe traumatic brain injuries in a work-related forklift truck accident in Oregon. ArLee fell into a deep coma, never to regain consciousness.

Raised as a Latter Day Saint in the homogenous Salt Lake City community, Marsha and her family immediately fell into their traditional religious rituals for healing, including fasting and prayers for complete recovery.

Marsha would travel every week-end from Salt Lake City to Oregon to visit her sister in the hospital. The two were very close, so the accident was devastating. Marsha would hold ArLee's hand, stroke her hair, massage her limbs. She'd carry on long, one-sided conversations, hoping for a response.

Nothing worked.

After three months and three brain surgeries, there was no noticeable change in ArLee's brain function, and her physical health was declining. She suffered bouts of pneumonia, pulmonary complications and the constant threat of infection. ArLee's physician recommended implanting a permanent tracheotomy and feeding tube, the first step in preparing ArLee for life suspended in a coma, for however long she lived.

Confronted with this grim prognosis, Marsha began a spiritual quest, opening herself up to new guidance that gave answers and comfort in a way she'd never found in her religious traditions, traditions she'd begun to question even before the tragedy. Holding her sister's hand for long hours, she experienced quiet, self-inspired meditations during which she asked herself and ArLee how she could best serve her. Rather than praying for her sister to be healed, she prayed for guidance and strength to do what was right for ArLee, just as she was, where she was.

Doing so reaped unexpected gifts. Though ArLee could not communicate in the customary way, Marsha felt her strong presence. Sitting in her sister's hospital room, Marsha entered a "holy place" she experienced as "being in the presence of pure light, pure being." Stripped of human personality, ego, or agenda, ArLee's spirit filled the room. ArLee also visited Marsha in her dreams, reassuring her that she was happy where she was and reminding Marsha to be happy in her life, to stay grounded even when ArLee wasn't there with her.

All of these things combined for Marsha into a growing sense of "inner knowing" that ArLee was already beyond earth, and no amount of prolonging her body's physical life artificially would bring the true ArLee back to them.

In response, Marsha asked her family and their church elders, who were fasting and praying for Arlee's return to health, to pray instead that "Thy will be done." Marsha wanted ArLee's highest good to be served. She met with ArLee's three adult children, and together they decided not to prolong Arlee's physical life with the recommended implants. Arlee died peacefully within hours of their decision.

After ArLee's death, Marsha committed to exploring this inner knowing she'd discovered. She sought and initiated formal practices in yoga and meditation. She enrolled in Maharashi International University to study Transcendental Meditation. Through regular daily practice, she learned to find her center of peace.

"Using a mantra was the easiest way for me to learn to meditate. You close your eyes, get into the silence, and begin repeating your mantra, slowly, mindfully. A mantra can be a simple, centering word, like 'Peace,' 'Love,' 'Breathe,' or 'Grace.' When a thought arises during meditation, as it most certainly will, you recognize it as a thought, then let it go easily and effortlessly, returning to your mantra. It is a clearing practice, allowing you to quiet your mind, let go of your thoughts or agenda, and open to Spirit."

These practices would serve her well in the coming weeks, as not one, but two sudden deaths would lead her to the brink of despair.

Tragedy has no respect for timing or fairness. Only eight weeks after losing ArLee, a knock on the door informed her that her beloved husband, Al, a pilot for a major airline and the picture of health, had suddenly died in Texas from a heart attack. He was fifty years old. Marsha collapsed at the crushing news. "When the doorbell rang, and the uniformed Chief Pilot introduced himself, it was as if the lights dimmed. You may call it shock or going into a dream state. I couldn't make a sound and I couldn't process the information. I just felt complete grief. And a part of me thought, 'There must be some mistake. He was fine when he wrapped me in his arms and kissed me good-bye. Oh, he must be on a hunting trip. I'll see him Monday.' Strangely, I signed my last love note to him with, 'Until we are together again.'

While still mourning her sister and husband, Marsha's father, Chris, unexpectedly passed away, six weeks after her husband. A third pillar in Marsha's life had crumbled. This time Marsha broke down completely. "I cannot do this," she remembers crying. "I can't continue in this world when the people I love most are leaving me behind."

Early, intense grief is often characterized by shock, numbness, disbelief, denial or intense pain. Some have described it as feeling like you're having open-heart surgery without the benefit of anesthesia. Others say you feel as though you're barely breathing, as if you're holding your head just above the surface of the water, yet wondering why you're even bothering to tread water at all. Why not just sink below the surface into true oblivion—anything to make the searing pain go away?

Marsha begged God to take her life. "Except for helping my grown children, who were also struggling with these sudden losses, I couldn't see a future here on earth. I couldn't see a reason to stay," Marsha reflects. "I told God, 'Please release me. Let me die, too, so I can join the people I love.'

But Marsha's desperate cry went unheeded. "Nobody leaves before their time, even when they want to. We did not choose our moment of birth, we do not choose our moment of death. But dying is not the worst thing," she reflects. "The worst thing is to hang around here, never having lived at all."

Many newly bereaved seek to escape in a myriad of ways: excessive sleep, over-activity, lethargy, food, shopping, TV, internet use, work, or drugs and alcohol. Anything to lessen the pain, even for a short while. Numbness has been called life's natural emotional shock absorber, enabling us to take in the reality and enormity of the loss a bit at a time, rather than all at once, allowing us to stay alive long enough to carry on. At some point, however, we must move past the numbness, ensuring we don't allow it to take hold as the defining aspect of our lives.

Struggling to hold on to life in a positive way, to release her pain and find meaning in what was left in her life, Marsha returned to the meditation and new spirituality she'd embarked on at her sister's bedside. During a meditation soon after her father's death, Marsha had a vision of her three departed loved ones. They stood erect, all in a row, like three tall Sequoia trees. They were smiling and excited, waiting in a staging area as if something wonderful was about to happen.

Marsha longed to join them, feeling like a tender young sapling in their presence, sensing they'd grown strong and moved well beyond her. She wondered if she'd have to wait for death to know what she sensed in them, an intense, profound spiritual power. This question fueled her continued commitment to grow spiritually through mediation and yoga. At that moment, she resolved to make her life a sincere quest to deepen her knowledge, her understanding and her expression of God's light and love, what she believes she saw in them.

"You need to cultivate and trust your inner knowing," says Marsha. "There is no shortcut to bypass the pain and agony of grieving your loss. But, ultimately you have a choice. You can choose to use the fear and sadness as a form of energy, propelling you into a more enlightened state of being. It took me a long time, and still today, I feel the tender heartache of missing my loved ones. But eventually, time is a great healer, if you allow it to be. If you awaken to love in this lifetime, wherever and however it is present, love and acceptance find you."

Marsha continued her graduate studies at Maharashi International University, completing courses in Conflict Resolution, Interfaith Relations and Peace Building. She lived in India for seven months studying under Hindu, Christian and Islamic instructors. She describes her current practice as Siddhi meditation, devoting at least an hour twice a day to the spiritual exercise. She attends several different churches regularly, enjoying the beauty in their similarities, the unity of their spiritual Truth. She refers to them as vehicles to "practice staying awake."

Today Marsha is an international interfaith activist and volunteer. She has traveled to thirty-seven countries, participating in conferences and initiatives promoting religious understanding, harmony and global cooperation to alleviate human suffering. She is active in United Religions Initiative, a worldwide organization that fosters religious tolerance and communication among the world's major religions. She opens her home to diverse religious and spiritual leaders who travel to Salt Lake City to participate in interfaith events.

During her daily meditation, she quiets her mind, sets aside her ego, and listens for the voice of Spirit to guide her. "Where would you have me go today, whom shall I see, and what shall I do to serve your voice of Love?" she asks.

She is unafraid of death. Marsha has helped seventeen people make their spiritual transition beyond this life, sharing her own divine light, assuring them that they are embarking on a wonderful new adventure. Though she doesn't actively seek this role, she has learned that her peaceful, serene presence and attitude make a difference at this fearful time, and she is generous with her time and spirit.

For Marsha, the answer to life's questions cannot be found "out there." Three painful losses compelled her to ask her own questions, find her own truths. "God dwells in the hearts of all people and in all religions. Everyone should be encouraged to practice his or her chosen religion or spiritual tradition. There are many paths up the mountain. We don't all have to take the same one. If we each walk our own path with love and authenticity, eventually we all find our way to the top.

"We are all God's children. Jesus was our brother. This is just as true for Muslims and Jews as it is for Christians. Ultimately, we all face the same question: What is my purpose for being here today? What is happening right here, right now that I can positively influence in love? Just remember that everything you see here, everything you experience here, is temporary. It won't last. Choose to live today expressing more love, more light. That's your gift to the world. Start with today. Give it away."

CHAPTER EIGHT

Laura

I grew up in the country, wandering the fields near my home. The brook and woods were my playground, the seasons my teacher. I spent hours sitting in my favorite apple tree reading books of mythology, fairy tales and far away lands. This tree provided me a safe quiet retreat from my often-nosey siblings and planted in me the seed of what would become my spirituality. Watching it through the seasons—from spring leaves, to abundant fruit, to bare stick and back again—taught me important lessons about nature's continuous cycle of renewal.

The tree also taught me about life's interconnectedness. Soft, sweet apple blossoms attracted insects, which pollinated the apple flowers and provided food for the birds. Autumn's fallen apples nourished the soil, which in turn sustained the tree through the bleak, cold winter. If one part of the cycle was disturbed, it affected the whole. A late cold snap in the spring could kill the young buds. No flowers meant fewer insects, which meant a weakened harvest as well as fewer, hungrier birds. One touch of the web of life causes a ripple that affects others well beyond the point of contact.

My parents were Episcopalian, but we left the church when I reached my teens. This break was actually a relief to me since I didn't feel a personal connection to the God of my parents. I saw him as an angry God, separate from his creation. Instead, as a young teen, I was drawn to the beauty and harmony of nature. I intuitively felt a sense of the divine feminine in the world around me, and a connection to a god that was gentle and protective. These deities were not transcendent from creation; they were instead immanent within the world. The earth and all life upon it were therefore sacred. Alone in the woods, I began creating rituals and practices to honor the Goddess, God, energy of the earth and the seasons.

I practiced my own form of prayer and ritualistic devotion until my mid-twenties, when I spontaneously shared my beliefs with a friend. "Oh, you're a Witch!" she exclaimed. At first I was taken aback. I didn't believe in evil forces, or in causing harm, my understanding of what that word represented. So how could I be a Witch? "No, not that kind of Witch," my friend explained. "It means you practice ancient, nature-based traditions. It's also known as Wicca."

With that, I found a new identity as well as a spiritual community that reflects my homegrown beliefs. I've been on the Wicca path ever since with others who share my ideas of divinity and spirituality. I felt so at home in Wicca, I decided to train as a clergy member. Today I lead a coven, teaching others the way of our Tradition. I am involved with both the academic and the ritualistic aspects of Neopagan practices.

Contrary to negative false images, Wicca (a form of Neo-Paganism—Neo differentiates between the practices of our ancestors and those of today) is a peaceful, harmonious and balanced way of thinking and living. It is often polytheistic and promotes oneness with the divine and all of creation. To a Wiccan, a Witch is a loving healer, teacher, seeker, giver and protector of all living things. This has been my calling, in remarkable ways that I could not have foreseen when I began this path. This is where my real story begins....

Having discovered Wicca and Neo-Paganism, I sought others of my faith. A poster in a bookstore advertised a Neo-Pagan weekend festival called Rites of Spring and despite living on a meager secretarial wage in Boston, I determined to find the funds to register for the event. Two nights before leaving, I experienced the strangest dream. In it, I saw myself join together with a man in the most loving, intimate embrace. Though I knew we'd never met, it was as if my soul already knew him and was coming home. At the time, I wasn't really dating and hadn't been interested in any relationships. I shrugged off the dream, nearly forgetting it by the time I arrived at the festival.

This was my first time at a Wiccan event. My body hummed with energy. I spent most of the first day exploring the environment and meeting new people. And then I met the man of my dreams. Literally.

When Peter offered to help me gather firewood, I was shocked. I recognized his dark blond hair, trimmed beard and intense blue eyes immediately. He was the man from my dream. While Peter hadn't experienced a prophetic dream, as I had, his reaction to me was similar. We shared an instant, powerful connection.

Peter was a serious, devoted Christian Pagan who had once practiced as a Hindu monk. He lived in New York City, five hours away from my Boston home. For three years we visited each other on weekends, giving ourselves the time and space we each needed to heal from past relationships. When our relationship reached a deeper level of commitment, I moved to New York to share an apartment with my beloved.

Three years later, on the anniversary of the day we first met, we were married at the Cathedral of St. John in New York, the ceremony presided over by both a Christian minister and a Wiccan priestess. Rather than the traditional bridal couple, our wedding cake was graced with a statue of Shakti & Shiva, the Hindu God and Goddess of love and creation. Surrounded by friends and family, and buoyed by their love and good wishes, we drove off on our honeymoon with high hopes for the future and the anticipation of starting our life and a family together.

Soon after, the dreams started. Peter was ill and dying ... sometimes he was dead. I'd wake up screaming and crying. Peter would pull me close, whispering words of comfort, "I'm right here ... I'm not going anywhere." But I knew something was wrong. Two months to the day after we were married, Peter was diagnosed with colon cancer.

We were stunned. Peter was a construction worker. He was lean, fit, muscled, an athletic vegetarian who'd followed a macrobiotic diet for more than 15 years. His family had no history of cancer. It made no earthly or divine sense!

At first, Peter rejected conventional treatment, including surgery, chemotherapy and radiation. Instead he sought macrobiotic healers and remedies. My disbelief turned to anger, both at the gods and goddesses that this was happening, and at Peter for stubbornly refusing medically proven treatment for his form of cancer.

For three months, I threw outrageous spiritual tantrums. I was an angry, screaming hateful person toward the God and Goddess. I even denounced their existences at times, or questioned their devotion to me. "How dare You?!" I'd rail. And I'd scream the same questions at Peter. Didn't he want to get well? Finally, Peter left to stay with his mother.

After a week of desperation and forced solitude, I found a place of peace and embraced the mystery of what was happening. I came to understand that there was something greater than myself in control, and I would have to either trust that universal force, or not. I decided to trust. It was not an easy, peaceful path of reconciliation. But that is part of the great mystery and beauty of life . . . while I disconnected myself from Them, They stayed connected to me.

This was an important lesson in my life. I accepted Peter's stubborn refusal to follow conventional medical protocol, and told him instead, "I don't understand what is happening or why, but I love you and will support you in whatever you decide to do." I opened up to whatever experiences the gods were handing me and let go of control. It was then that Peter announced he would, reluctantly, schedule the recommended surgery and treatments.

I stayed overnight in the hospital the day he had surgery, holding his hand and wishing him strength. When I finally came home, exhausted, I found the statue of Shakti and Shiva, our wedding cake topper, shattered on the floor. I swept up the pieces and, in a state of panic, tried frantically to glue them together. But like our future, it was fractured beyond repair.

Test results from the surgery came back indicating the cancer had spread to his lymph nodes. We started down the road of medical intervention and hope. Perhaps it was his stubbornness to act sooner, or maybe just his fate—whatever the reason, the cancer refused to relinquish him. After two years of fighting, trying every possible medical, physical and spiritual method, he was labeled terminal.

We visited my family in western Massachusetts for our second anniversary. My brother and his wife lived on a commune in the country and were expecting their first child. To our joy and surprise, my niece made an early arrival in time to meet her aunt and uncle during our visit. I watched with tears in my eyes as she emerged into the world to take her first breath. Here before me was a reminder of the other side of the cycle of life. What a gift the God and Goddess had given me! This beautiful promise that, just as things must die, life also begins again. It is the constant turning of the wheel we call life.

Peter and I returned to New York with regret. We both felt a deep connection to the land and to my family. I wanted to give Peter a last gift—a place where he could live out his final days in deep connection to love and nature. I also wanted to provide him full-time home care so that he could die with dignity. I could not see how this was possible, but I begged in my heart to my God and Goddess, "Please, I need help."

Two months later, on a return visit to my brother and his family, a neighbor announced that the house next door to the commune was available for rent. Our prayers had been answered. With help from family and friends, we packed up our belongings and moved.

Peter lived for one more year, at peace among the trees, fields and rolling hills of the commune. His weight dropped from 225lbs to a mere 115, but to the amazement of his hospice caregivers, he was still walking, and even worked on the house up to the day before he died. He was conscious to his last breath.

I was alone with Peter during the final moments of his life. He swiped at his blanket and attempted to get up, asking someone I couldn't see, "Where are we going?" I asked him what he saw and he told me, between gasps of breath, that there were three men in the room who had come for him. I realized he was dying and it was time for him to go. Panic gripped me, but I took a deep breath and centered myself, allowing peace to settle in and around me.

I knew Peter was worried about what would happen to me after he died, so I took his hands and kissed him one last time. Somehow I mustered the inner strength to comfort him, to pull myself together enough to send him off in peace and love, even though I would fall apart later.

I told him I loved him and that it was OKfor him to go. I reminded him I was surrounded by people who loved me, that I had family and friends who would take care of me after he was gone. I held my beloved husband through the final moments of his life. As his systems shut down, I whispered to him again and again, "Sweetheart, I love you, I love you, I love you." I sent him on his way with my love. Pagans believe there is a veil between the worlds of life and death. I am certain that on that day, it parted for Peter, and with the guidance of his three guardians, he passed through to his new existence.

After his death, Peter visited my dreams, checking in to reassure me all was well. Once, in a moment of deep grief, I created a sacred space and talked to him, out loud, as if he was in the room. I cried and shared memories for about an hour, ending with, "Good night, sweetheart." A number of Peter's journals were in the room, items so private I couldn't bring myself to go through them. At that moment, I had the intuitive urge to pick one of his journals off the shelf and open it. The page contained two words, in Peter's handwriting: "Good Night."

I cried, joyfully, reaffirmed that while life in its present form is temporary, life in a new form continues on.

A new existence awaited me, as well. At first it was survival and healing. Then, a new path of love.

Tom and I met through a mutual friend, while Peter was sick. He had recently lost his mother to heart disease and understood the pain and grief I was going through. Tom would collect and deliver food that friends had made for us, and would sit for hours with me while I processed these feelings. In fact, Tom was in the house when Peter died and heard my agonized screams. He held me for what seemed like hours, and stayed with me as I worked through the initial shock and trauma of Peter's death. He cared for me like you would a child until I was more able to function.

Six months later, Tom told me he loved me, but I wasn't ready to hear him. At first, I refused to see him, but he quietly wooed me, always giving me space to grieve, heal and grow. A year after Peter died, we began to officially date.

After a while, I realized I loved Tom. Not like I loved Peter. Loving Peter was all-consuming. It was as if we knew on some level that our time together was limited and we devoured each moment with an intensity I never knew possible.

Love with Tom was solid, nurturing, slow and steady. He took care of me. He was always there for me. He made me feel secure and happy.

Four years after Peter's death, we were married.

Marriage to Tom brought the possibility of another dream I'd thought lost—motherhood! Excited by the prospect of a family, we tried again and again. No luck. We entered into the frustrating and heartbreaking world of fertility treatments, with no success.

Again, I screamed to my Deities, "Why? What is the lesson here?"

Tom and I felt strongly that we were meant to create a family, but nothing was happening. Instead of months of tantrums, I quickly opened myself up to the experience and asked the Goddess and God for guidance. We looked into adoption. Tom and I spent months poring over websites and attending adoption events, waiting for something to tell our hearts where our child was. The answer came during an adoption fair when someone casually suggested we look at Cambodia. One glance at these children and we knew. We immediately registered with an adoption agency. Just as we finished the home study paperwork allowing us to adopt, the US froze adoptions from Cambodia.

Undeterred, we registered with the Department of Social Services. I requested a newborn, wanting an infant experience. At first our Wicca beliefs were an obstacle. We spent hours with the licensed social worker on our case, teaching her about our belief system, dispelling common myths about Wicca. We explained how our religion is based on loving and respecting the planet and all creatures; working towards creating harmony and balance in life; and above all, doing no harm. Convincing her that we could offer an infant a loving home full of kindness, respect, responsibility and caring took time and patience, but the effort was well worth it. We were approved!

And then, we waited.

On the last day of January, on the night before a major Wiccan holiday celebrating "new beginnings," the social worker called. She had an emergency case—a 5-year-old boy that needed placement for the weekend. Would we be willing? We agreed to take care of him until Monday, when they would find him a long-term placement.

He arrived. And broke our hearts.

He was small for his age, with eyes full of pain. He suffered night terrors and fear of abandonment. Little wonder after 14 foster placements in his short life!

We spent the night with him, gave him a flashlight, talked and sang to him. We held his hands and rubbed his back until he slept. By Monday, we knew he was meant to be our son. He wasn't an infant—he was five and that was fine by us.

We requested and were granted placement and we learned

he had a 3-year-old sister. On Summer Solstice, six months later, she joined our family.

And don't think the guidance of the God and Goddess went unheeded.

Two months later, the agency from Cambodia notified us we could adopt. They had a 4-year-old girl available. Did we want her? We answered with a loud, "Yes!" The following January our Cambodian daughter arrived. Our family was complete.

The challenges and joys of parenting have changed me. By teaching and modeling the principles of my religion to my children, I deepen my faith. In our home, we maintain sacred space and have created a family altar. We bless our meals, light candles and celebrate special holidays together, connecting us to each other and to all of creation.

Through all my journeys, I have come to understand that life is full of transition and transformation. Sometimes this is a gentle process but often it is rough, loud, and difficult. At times, happiness seems impossible. The advice I give to others is to allow transition to deepen you, to transform you. Allow the universe to unfold in the great mystery. The woman I was with Peter died with him. I am a transformed person, physically, mentally and spiritually. I no longer fight with the present, even if it is painful.

While I may still question or get angry with my Deities when life is difficult, I also give Them thanks. I stay present in the moment instead of trying to control the future. I look for the joy that can be found, even within the deepest places of despair, because I know the wheel will turn and this too, this moment, will end.

Just as I am sure another—filled with new possibilities— will begin.

CHAPTER NINE

Elizabeth

Elizabeth, a convert to Christianity who works as a life coach for others, knows first-hand the strength and comfort faith can bring in a crisis. "I made the decision to convert when I was forty years old, after a period of searching for something more spiritually meaningful. I had a vision of being enveloped in Christ's arms, from the back. All I needed to do to convert was to turn around and take Him into my heart.

"I think of Christ as a rock, an image that's been very meaningful to me throughout my Christian walk. I had been abused as a child, and coming to know Christ as trustworthy, steadfast and faithful was very important. I think of my faith in Him as basic, simple, personal, trusting and child-like."

She believes the spiritual relationship she'd nurtured over the years became a true rock for her on the longest, worst night of her life, giving her the strength to survive it and the grace to take the first steps toward accepting it and moving forward.

Elizabeth's daughter Margaret was a Ph.D. in molecular biology, a graduate of Emory Medical School, where she met and married her husband John, who was also a medical student. "They referred to themselves as two bio-nerds who met and fell in love," Elizabeth recalls fondly. By February 2001, they had two beautiful sons, Bentley, 8, and Davis, 5. John had a full-time medical practice in Auburn, California. They were a young, healthy, athletic family, on their way to the mountains for a vacation.

They left their Auburn home on Friday night headed toward Washington, but Margaret didn't feel well, so they stopped earlier than expected at a motel in Shasta City. John put her to bed. If she felt better in the morning, they'd continue on. If not, they'd return home.

Margaret did not feel better. In fact, she woke up extremely ill and John rushed her to the nearest hospital, where she was diagnosed with a serious strep B infection that they couldn't fight. By late Saturday, Margaret had been transported to a larger Medical Center in Redding, and her infection had turned toxic. John knew she might not survive.

He called their shocked family members. "You should come," he told them. "She's fighting for her life. She may not make it."

It took a few phone calls to Elizabeth for the reality to sink in. How could this be happening, when less than twenty-four hours earlier, her daughter had been happily packing for a vacation? The hospital staff administered powerful antibiotics, but the infection was resistant. Margaret went into septic shock, where the circulatory system shuts down and the body can't get enough oxygen to survive.

It was the longest, darkest night of Elizabeth's life. Like any mother, she desperately wanted to be at her gravely ill daughter's bedside, but she couldn't get there. She'd recently moved to rural Southern Oregon, hundreds of miles from Redding and a treacherous drive over two mountain passes, especially for Elizabeth who suffers from poor night vision.

Worse yet, a storm moved in. Attempting the drive would be a risk to her own safety. "I thought of asking for help from the church I'd just started attending, but I could only remember the name of the pastor and one other woman. I called them, but it was late at night, and no one answered."

So she waited. "It's all I could do. I was alone, nineteen miles from town and I didn't know anyone who lived near me. The phone was my lifeline. After my daughters Kate and Porter reached the hospital, they'd call and tell me what medical procedures they were trying."

Alone and out of touch, Elizabeth experienced a range of emotions. "It felt like I was in a play and acting out the role of a mother who couldn't reach her dying child. Intellectually, I knew what was happening, but I didn't fully experience the depth of the crisis. C.S. Lewis once said, 'Denial is the shock absorber for the soul.' Denial was one of the ways that God was getting me through the night."

But she was aware enough to know she needed help to deal with what was happening hundreds of miles away. If she couldn't get it from friends or neighbors, she knew she could turn to her faith. "It felt like I was in a deep, dark pit. It was cold and terrifying, but my feet were firmly planted on the rock of Jesus Christ. As difficult as it was to wait through the storm, He was not going to allow me to drown.

"So there I sat through the long dark night, my head scarcely above water. No matter what transpired, I knew Jesus would get me through. I sat upright in bed, and wrapped myself in a quilt, tactilely feeling the arms of Jesus around me. I said to myself over and over, 'Remember, breathe.' Then I would consciously breathe in the life-giving spirit of Christ, and exhale all of my terror and fear. I stayed like that until 3:00 am when they called to tell me Margaret was gone.

"Later that morning, I finally reached an older couple from church, and they arranged for a young woman to drive me to the hospital, several hours away."

The first year after a loved one dies is often the most difficult. As a life coach, Elizabeth is aware of this and brought the same compassionate assistance to her own experience that she would give to a client. She took a sabbatical when she found herself struggling to stay present for her clients. She attended Compassionate Friends, a local grief group for parents who have lost children, and met with a grief counselor. Still, it was a painful and difficult year. She moved into town to be closer and to feel more connected.

Her new church was a godsend, confirmation of her faith that Christ would take care of her. "They barely knew me, but they wrapped their collective arms around me and carried me through the first year. It was a gift."

And she took deliberate steps toward health and healing. "After Margaret's death, I resisted the impulse to isolate, and I would make myself go out into the community. Exercise was very important. Walking has always been a part of my daily routine, and it kept me out of depression. I took up painting. I made a memory book of Margaret with photos, her favorite sayings, letters etc. I would take it out often and cherish my memories of her.

"I read a lot of grief books. Some were good, and some were trite. I found that people sometimes say the strangest things to you after you've lost a loved one. Well-meaning Christians would offer me platitudes such as 'God must have really needed Margaret, because He called her home so soon.' Or some would ask me, 'Well, was Margaret saved?' implying that it was OK if she died as long as she accepted Christ as her personal Savior, but unforgivable if she had died 'unsaved.'

For me, it was painful to lose Margaret, whether or not she was 'saved.' People don't know what to say to you, so you have to learn to accept their fumbling words as well-intentioned and let go of any negative interpretations."

Never underestimate the power of compassionate listening in the grief process. Early on, Elizabeth had the opportunity to tell and retell the story of Margaret's life and death to two housemates, both of whom are Christians. One had lost her son when he was twenty-one; both volunteered at nursing homes and had years of experience dealing with death and dying. They listened, and listened and listened, another great gift of love and patience for which Elizabeth is grateful.

"Two 'God' interventions helped me after Margaret's death," Elizabeth adds, "involving people who shared their septic shock experiences with me. The first woman had septic shock, and came close to dying. She told me that she never realized she was nearly dying, and she was never afraid. This was very comforting to me, since Margaret had a tube down her throat and couldn't communicate. We really didn't know what she was going through. I like to think that she just lost consciousness and never knew she was dying, until Jesus welcomed her into His arms.

"Another young woman I met lost her sister to a similar infection. But, unlike Margaret who died very suddenly, her unfortunate sister died by slow, dreadful degrees over 6 months, enduring gangrene and amputations. I never had a chance to say goodbye to Margaret, but I also didn't have to watch her suffer a prolonged, painful death.

"Both of these women offered me some peace in the experience of losing my daughter, another gift from God."

Elizabeth used a variety of spiritual tools to re-engage in life and keep her afloat. "I never once asked 'Why?' I did not get angry with God. Even though I didn't understand, and I was numb with grief over losing Margaret, I had a deep sense of peace that God was in control. I always felt 'The Rock' under my feet."

Since losing Margaret, Elizabeth's faith has deepened and become more real. "I moved even more from having an intellectual faith to a simple child-like faith based on trusting God. I concentrate on God's presence in nature, and experiencing Him through the five senses, on 'feeling, seeing, and hearing' His presence all around me. This is particularly powerful for me in the change of seasons, and especially during spring, when all that seemed dead is born anew. It is important to maintain a close, personal relationship with God and I find this easiest to do when I am in touch with nature.

"I have created healing rituals for myself. I look up at the stars at night and say a prayer for Margaret and her family. I put aside quiet time each morning to journal. Each day, I write about what is going on in my life and how I feel about it. And I make a point to write five things for which I am grateful. These days, they are mainly about relationships and experiencing God in the beauty around me. This is a very helpful practice I started in 1990 when my marriage crumbled. I could process things quietly, and express my feelings in a safe place, which has served me well since losing my child.

"Finally, I participate in a weekly women's Bible study. Meeting to pray and study the Scriptures has been a vital part of my life, perhaps the single most important activity for my spiritual health since losing Margaret. Through everything, I always maintain my vision of Christ holding out His arms to me; being held in His arms in times of despair and desperation has remained a meaningful metaphor."

Sometimes healing happens in unexpected ways. "I went

to stay with John and Margaret's boys the week after she died and I found her flannel bathrobe—a big black watch plaid robe that she wore when she got up in the morning. I wrapped myself up in it while I was there, because her scent was still in it and that comforted me. I asked John if I could take it home with me and he reluctantly agreed. I also took a white fleece jacket I'd given her years before that she liked to wear. In the coming weeks, months and years, these two garments offered me a sense of closeness to my daughter. When I really missed her, I would wrap myself up in her robe. Eventually, I needed that less and less, and the jacket and robe slowly worked their way to the back of my closet.

"Last fall, God gave me an idea. I made black and white patchwork pillows out of the robe fabric and gave one to each of my grandsons, and one to each of my daughters. Inside the pillow's zipper, I laminated a brief note. The note told them about the pillow, what it had been made of, and what it represented. By snuggling up to it, they could be reminded of Margaret's essence, and how much she continued to love them every day. When I gave them to my grandsons, they didn't say a word, but took the pillows to their room, so I wasn't sure how they felt about them. But both boys insisted on bringing their pillows to camp this past summer. I believe that Margaret is still a loving presence in their lives today and the pillows help them remember her."

Elizabeth has simple advice for those whose grief is new. "Get counseling and join a grief support group. Take the time that YOU need to grieve; there is no predetermined timeframe. Don't let people rush you through the process. Be extraordinarily gentle with yourself. Treat yourself with the gentle love of an adoring grandmother. Ask yourself, 'What would my gentle *Oma* say to me right now?'

"Also, I read and re-read the Psalms. I personalize them. A few of my favorites are:"

Psalm 40:1-3, NLT (New Living Translation)

I waited patiently for the Lord to help me, and He turned and heard my cry. He lifted me out of the pit of despair, out of the mud and mire. He set my feet on solid ground and steadied me as I walked along. He has given me a new song to sing, a hymn of praise to our God.

Psalm 62:2 NLT

I wait quietly before God for my salvation comes from Him. He alone is my rock and my salvation, my fortress where I will not be shaken.

Psalm 62:2 TM (The Message)

He's the solid rock under my feet, breathing room for my soul. An impregnable castle. I'm set for life.

As a life coach, Elizabeth knows it takes work and commitment to heal. As a Christian, she firmly believes in God's loving spirit to help us bear the things that seem unbearable. He will help us at the times it seems impossible to help ourselves. Recently, in her morning quiet time, Elizabeth asked God what simple message she might share about her painful experience and her healing process. In opening her daily devotional, she found this verse for the day:

Psalm 62:2. "God is good."

CHAPTER TEN

Barbara & Kathy

Listening to Barbara and her daughter, Kathy, and seeing the obvious peace and acceptance on their faces, it is hard to believe they have endured so much.

"I am 84 years old," begins Barbara. "When I look back on our family life, I see us as a large, happy, fun, spirited, social and busy family. I know that sounds odd. One might expect to find a long traumatic trail of tears filled with anguish and depression, given what we've endured. But honestly, it wasn't like that. We had five children: Doug, Kathy (our only daughter), David, Richard and James. We weren't religious, though we believed in the values of honesty, love, compassion, hard work and patience. We were there for each other and we knew how to have fun. Well into adulthood, the kids would gather for holidays, referred to as "Borg laugh-ins" (our family's last name). We entertained each other for days, repeating favorite family stories and laughing as if we'd never heard the punch line before. That was the distinguishing characteristic of our family. We thoroughly enjoyed each other's company.

"I shared a special bond with my youngest son, James. We

called him Jamie. He was the love of my life. I could not imagine a boy more loved, or more loveable. He was a very happy child—fun-loving, athletic, quick witted, adventurous and social."

Kathy cuts in quietly. "Mom did have a special bond with him, but the whole family adored him. He was 'our boy,' the youngest, the one we kind of helped raise and felt invested in. I was 13 years old when he was born, so I adopted him, mothering and hen-pecking the poor boy at every opportunity. He was handsome, charming, and sensitive. What was there not to love? We all spent a lot of time with him, since Mom and Dad both worked. I cannot emphasize enough how much we loved Jamie. He was the apple of all our eyes."

"There was no hint of depression when Jamie was young," Barbara reflects. "Looking back, I noticed some changes in him around puberty. But at the time, they didn't signal anything out of the ordinary. I'd already raised three sons and one daughter through the tumultuous teenage years, and James seemed normal. I attributed any odd behavior to typical teenage rebellion, hormones and his need to define himself as an individual, unique from his siblings. But one distinct memory of that time has stuck in my mind. At one point he completely stopped smiling. For an entire family vacation to New York City, he wore overalls and refused to smile for any of the pictures."

It was the late 60's. Depression, therapy, suicide prevention, mental health—these terms barely existed at the time, and certainly not for public discussion.

"When Jamie was 18 years old, he took an overdose of pills and was rushed to the hospital," Kathy continues. "I was shocked. How could this happen? I don't remember much of that traumatic day. I know the doctors were worried that there might be brain damage from the drugs and I was terrified that we wouldn't ever have Jamie back as we knew him.

"Thankfully, he didn't suffer any brain damage and he slowly recovered. We were so grateful. I remember sobbing over him, holding him close to my heart, and begging him, 'Promise me Jamie that you will never ever do this again.' Once Jamie regained his health, my mom scheduled him visits with a highly-respected local psychiatrist. He attended regular therapy sessions and was put on anti-depressants. We rarely spoke to him about it, but we worried incessantly and whispered all the time to each other about how to help him. We didn't know what to do, except to keep hyper vigilant around him. We watched for signs of depression, anxiety, irritation or anything other than smiles. We did the only thing that we knew to do at the time. We told him we loved him, many times a day."

For Barbara, life became a nightmare. "I worried day and night. I would call Jamie from work, just to hear his voice. I would pray at night, asking God to surround my son with a divine layer of protection, asking for the wisdom to know what to do, how to mother a boy who almost took his own life. One day I called from work, again and again, and there was no answer. I was frantic. I rode the bus home, praying to myself, 'Please God, please, let him live.' I rushed through the front door and raced through the house in a panic. I couldn't find him. I finally spotted him in the backyard, mowing the lawn. He hadn't heard the phone calls. I ran out to him and crushed him in a hug. He looked at me like I was crazy. And I suppose I was crazy, in a way.

"I couldn't shake my anxiety and I didn't know how to help James. I tried to work through these things with my husband, but that was not his way. He was a good, kind, hard-working man, but he came from a stoic, Scandinavian background. He wasn't one to share emotions, and he couldn't tolerate anyone else being overly expressive. We were never able to bond that way. But I was able to find release and reassurance with my daughter, Kathy. I guess that's why God gave me a daughter. I could wear my heart on my sleeve with her, and not be judged for it. That emotional safe haven gave me some respite from the perpetual worry.

"Jamie resumed a normal high school life. He played, studied, worked part-time, hung out with friends, played in a band, had girlfriends. He never acted depressed; in fact, quite the contrary. He was handsome, popular and engaged in life, and he avoided noticeably destructive substances, like drugs or alcohol. He was often the 'designated driver,' concerned with getting his friends home safely, even at the height of the rock & roll drug culture of that time.

"When he was 21, James became involved in a very unhealthy romantic relationship. She was needy, sad, overly dependent, someone today that we might call 'high maintenance.' I never understood the dynamics of the relationship and I couldn't be happy about it, but he was an adult. He had to make his own choices.

"On May 24, 1981, his girlfriend called, asking if we had seen James. My heart sank. I knew something had happened.

"James vanished without a trace. After a fight, his girlfriend had asked him to leave. He didn't pack anything, leave a note, or contact anyone. When I realized he hadn't even take his contact solution, I think I knew he was gone for good. Nonetheless, for six months we searched for him. We called everyone we could think of; we wandered through the mountains and rivers near our home, places James loved. We soothed ourselves by making up stories about what happened, pretending that he had bolted this life and set up somewhere as a hermit. The alternative was too much to bear."

Kathy continues, "We were crazy with fear and anxiety. We hired psychics. We spent all of our free time searching for him. At one point my parents even bought a trailer, planning to hit the road to look. Back then, the police ignored missing persons, especially adults. So we were on our own, and we were relentless. The psychics reassured us—Jamie was still alive, living among rocks, trees and nature. But what they meant by 'alive' was very different from our understanding. Or what we hoped for."

Even in this tumultuous time, Barbara sought comfort in her own form of spirituality. "I read and meditated constantly. If I wasn't looking for him, I was trying to connect with him in my meditation. I studied Edgar Cayce to learn how to communicate telepathically. I transmitted strong, loving, positive messages to him. 'You are so loved. You are strong. You are healthy. Your family loves you. I love you. We miss you. Please come home.' I believed that if he was alive and I maintained a constant, loving, telepathic connection, he might eventually return home.

"Six months later, two boys found a body next to a creek near our home. When we heard, we went to the police station and explained our situation. They showed us a beautiful pocket watch found on the body and at that moment we knew. It was James' graduation gift. Ultimately, they made sure with James' dental records. Even then, I remember asking our dentist to please tell me it was all a cruel mistake, but he couldn't, of course. It was James. He'd overdosed on drugs."

"After Jamie died," Kathy reflects, "we hunkered down in survival mode, performing the most minimal tasks to get through the day. We cried, we second-guessed, we raged. 'What did we miss? What did this mean, or that? What could we have done differently?' We learned that Jamie had taken himself off his anti-depressants. Why? No one had any answers. His psychiatrist could only share that sometimes a person starts to feel better and decides they don't need them anymore. It was a heart-wrenching, horrifying situation, and we couldn't change anything about it. And it was so hard to move forward."

Not surprisingly, Jamie's death hit Barbara particularly hard. "It took me a long, long time to feel alive again. I was hanging on by a thin thread, even with the love and support of my family as a reason to get out of bed in the morning. A year later, a dear friend who had lost his baby to SIDS invited me to hear a speaker, Wally Minto, whose approach helped him accept his baby's death. It was the first time since losing James that I felt any desire to leave the house. I asked my daughter-in-law, Susie, to come with me, but I had no expectations that this speaker, or anyone or anything else, would help.

"To my great surprise, Wally introduced me to what would become a life-long spiritual path for healing. Remember, we were not a religious family. Growing up, I'd seen so many self-described 'religious' people, acting in hurtful, judgmental and selfish ways, completely hypocritical to their espoused teachings. Wally called his process Alpha Awareness, and it included quieting the mind, opening the heart, and allowing a loving, non-judgmental presence into your being, just like meditation. I practiced these principles, and for the first time since James' death, I felt moments of peace. Susie and I, encouraged by our budding spirituality and inner peace, took up Wally's teaching with great enthusiasm. It eventually led me to study A Course in Miracles (ACIM), which continues to this day to be my main spiritual path.

"I don't know how I would have survived losing James if I hadn't found ACIM. In study groups, often with Susie, and in private prayer and meditation, I realized that I had a genuine choice about how to respond to James' death. At any given moment, I could choose to perceive him, and his physical absence, through the eyes of love, or through the eyes of fear and attachment to what could have, should have been true, according to my limited perception. I learned to distinguish between the things I have control and influence over, like myself, my way of being at any given moment, and the things I have no control over, like Jamie's life choices. Love brought me peace; fear brought me terror and deep remorse. Slowly at first, then more and more, I chose love.

"When I look back on Jamie's short life, I know in my heart that I was a good mother. I wasn't perfect, but I couldn't have showered him with any more love, care and attention than I did. We were very close. I loved him completely, every cell of his being. I understand now that I did everything I could. Today, in the present moment, I have to love myself enough to exist here, to resist the urge to replay the past to get answers. There aren't any."

A Course in Miracles, at heart, is a spiritual path that encourages the practitioner to accept what is, to release oneself through internal and external forgiveness, from guilt, anger, and other negative emotions, especially in situations that one cannot control. This path served the mother and daughter well, even as they experienced more tragic suffering.

"David, my third child, took his life thirteen years after Jamie, when he was 46 years old. By all outward appearances, David was very successful. A talented workaholic engaged in the large and difficult remodel of the Joseph Smith Memorial Building, a Salt Lake City landmark, he often worked 16-hour days. His skill and diligence earned him a big promotion. Handsome and charming, he had many close friends; he was athletic and exercised regularly. He was devoted to his two children, a daughter Emily and a son we called 'little David,' and spent all of his free time with them. But his marriage ended in divorce, a blow he had a hard time overcoming.

"Years after his divorce, David fell in love with Kathleen, a beautiful younger woman. As was his way, he fell hard for her, and lavished her with gifts and attention. They seemed happy together and he bought a house for them, but it didn't last. Eventually Kathleen kicked him out. Devastated, he begged her to take him back. When she refused, David began to chain smoke and drink beer. Dejected and alone, he used beer to medicate his shattered feelings, and the cigarettes to keep him distracted from his pain. But it wasn't enough. At midnight, April 20, 1994, David shot himself with a semi-automatic gun he'd bought a few days earlier."

"Growing up, David was my hero," Kathy comments. "Unlike Jamie, we knew that he was in trouble and tried everything to help him, to no avail. When Kathleen broke up with him, he threatened to kill himself if she didn't take him back. I begged him to move in with me, but he refused. He was seeing a therapist and taking anti-depressants. We offered to help him any way we could think of—emotionally, financially or spiritually. He always refused. We stood by helplessly as he spiraled into the dark abyss of depression."

"During Christmas and New Year's he was exhausted, lonely, and depressed. He spoke openly of his despair. It was around that time that he began acting in ways that hinted at what he was planning, but we either didn't know about it in advance, or we didn't understand. He gave permission to his ex-wife's new husband to adopt his children. He changed his life insurance policy to include Kathleen. He started giving away clothes and possessions to people he loved. He, too, took himself off his anti-depressants and stopped seeing his therapist.

"When he shot himself, I was so angry, and I felt so hurt and guilty. He was my brother, only two years younger than I. We'd been so close and I couldn't help him. In my rage, I confronted both his therapist, who was shocked and horrified at what he'd done, and the store that sold him the gun, demanding a full refund, since it had only been fired once—the shot that took my brother's life.

"Of course, I realized later that I was furious with David. How could he do that to us, especially when he knew what we'd been through after Jamie? And I was angry at myself, for letting it happen. But I also realized that none of us could have stopped David. He had to stop himself.

"After David's death, Mom and I attended a Suicide Survivor's group facilitated by a caring, sympathetic therapist who had lost her husband to suicide. In that room, my mom and I held each other and sobbed. We watched other parents and siblings who had survived a loved one's suicide. Their experiences and strength gave us hope. Still, the question lingered, 'What are we supposed to do or learn from losing Jamie and David this way? How do we heal from their actions and our terrible loss?' We knew we couldn't take years and years to heal from David's death, as we had with Jamie's. Eventually, with a lot of anguish and 'grief work,' we began to reconcile our loss.

"I knew that mom and I were healing when we slowly shifted to being the experienced ones helping the newest members, those who had just suffered a loved one's suicide. Allowing them to express their rage, guilt and horror, making them feel listened to and understood, we saw ourselves in them, and understood the progress we had made."

For Barbara, David's loss also meant continuing on the path of acceptance, even in the face of nearly unbearable sorrow. "We turned again to things we had learned from Wally Minto, and ACIM, especially that forgiveness is essential. Without forgiveness, you can't fully embrace life again. Even at David's services I approached Kathleen, the object of his unrequited passion, to let her know it was not her fault, that she was not to blame for David's choices. Guilt is a sign that you have not forgiven yourself. I sometimes say that I feel guilty that I don't feel guilty. Does that make sense? I feel tremendous sorrow, but I do not feel guilt.

"One of my favorite quotes from ACIM is 'I know nothing.' Boy, is that the truth! I try not to impose my perceptions on people or their actions. I understand that whatever reason or motive I make up for someone else's action is merely my projection. It's not real. I have learned not to torture myself by asking, 'Why?' There is no answer to that question that brings me inner peace, so I've decided to drop the question. 'Why?' 'Because that's what happened.' David took his life, that's why. No additional story required. Any 'answer' that you come up with to 'Why?' would merely be your own projection, your own terror story. We cannot know a loved one's heart and mind, especially not in the moment they pulled the trigger."

Barbara has tried to bring this message of love and acceptance to her children and grandchildren, to offer them the same peace that she has found. David's children had a hard time accepting their father's suicide. "Emily, twenty-three when David died, asked me, 'Why did my dad do this? Didn't he want to live to see my children, his grandchildren, one day?'

"Her questions tore at my heart, especially when I knew there was no answer. I could only explain that depression is a like a deep dark hole, and people suffering from it have no rational basis for what they think or do. Often they can't see past their own dark despair. They have very little energy for even the simplest tasks in life. Though we know it makes no sense, they take their lives because they believe that their loved ones will be better off with them gone. Little David, a teenager at the time, didn't speak about his dad for years. When he finally did, he chose to remember all the fun they had together, camping, shooting targets, hiking, setting off rockets. 'I miss him,' he added sweetly. 'Yes, me too,' I nodded."

Kathy has used ACIM, and more recently, Byron Katie's inquiry process in her book, *Loving What Is,* to help cope with her brothers' suicides, as well as trouble with her own daughter. "Ashley is twenty-two. She's had a rough ride so far. We almost lost her to drugs a few years ago. Depression and anxiety runs in our family, can you tell? We need to be constantly vigilant, proactive about treating it at the first sign. Ashley got hooked on crystal methamphetamine. From January to April of 2001, she cut off all her hair, quit school, quit showering, and came close to dying from drug use. She took anything and everything she could get her hands on, as long as needles weren't involved.

"Using tough love, I kicked Ashley out of the house. I told her she had to shape up or she couldn't stay. Her 'crazy-making' was making us all crazy. It was the hardest thing I've ever done, knowing that my daughter might well wind up living on the streets, or worse. It was a bold expression of love, a huge step for both of us. I packed her bags and sent her away. She wandered around for a few days, then came back, full of remorse and promises to shape up. She acknowledged she had a drug problem beyond her control, and needed help. I supported her recovery, not her using. I sent her to a good drug rehabilitation program, and she grasped the essentials of what she needed to do to live a clean, sober and happy life.

"Recently, I attended a women's ACIM retreat where I worked Byron Katie's inquiry process about my fear of losing Ashley. The process allowed me to accept the reality that I do not have control over Ashley's choices, now or in the future. All I can do is to love her unconditionally, in the moment."

Living in the moment is a central theme to many spiritual paths, as is unconditional love.

For Barbara and Kathy, A Course in Miracles has allowed them to survive and to believe in the constant presence of love in their lives, despite what might seem like evidence to the contrary. David and Jamie still exist for them, as does Barbara's husband, who died a few years ago from cancer. They both speak of dreams and meditations where they connect with these men, and of the playful, loving relationships they still maintain in their hearts and minds.

"I know Jamie, David and my husband all live in another world, quite happily," Barbara notes. "Jamie visits me in my dreams, which I find very comforting. I also have meditations I use to connect with his spirit. I guess you could call it a form of channeling, being receptive to your loved one's energy and listening for his message. I know some people would dismiss the idea that we can communicate with deceased loved ones, but I am open and receptive to learning from them. Jamie always reminds me that this life is only about learning how to love. Nothing else matters.

"My husband was skeptical of my spiritual pursuits while he was alive. But since his passing, he has told me, "You and Susie were right—love is all that matters." I have come to understand that different people hear or receive love in different ways. Perhaps that's why humans have so many religions and faith traditions! We're all uniquely configured to receive love's message through different means."

"And we're all spiritual works in progress," adds Kathy. "I try to remind myself of that with my daughter, especially. So far, Ashley has chosen not to return to drugs. I encourage her to nourish her soul, in a way that is authentic for her. We read Unity's *Daily Word* together, and she has begun her own spiritual quest. I know how valuable this is, how much my own spiritual journey has helped me survive.

"I'm a very different person today because of the loss of my brothers. I'm so very grateful every day for every thing, every person, even the smallest of things. I spend each day literally counting my blessings. I realize now how temporary it can all be. I find joy in the moment."

CHAPTER ELEVEN

Victoria

Looking back over the past twenty years, Victoria is astounded at how different the life she's lived is from the life she expected. As a young, educated Catholic newlywed couple, she and Steve had everything going for them. Good jobs with better opportunities, a home filled with love and faith, and every hope for the natural course of family and children.

But God had other plans.

After years of dealing with the anguish of not being able to have their own children, Victoria and Steve looked into adoption. By 1993, they were the loving parents of Christopher, age 3, and Ryan, 5. Victoria's rigorous medical education and position as the Associate Director of Pharmacy at Children's Hospital of Orange County, California, as well as Steve's education and professional position, made them an excellent placement home for children, and offered Victoria a certain amount of confidence in at least the health aspect of parenting.

In August, when 3-year-old Chris contracted chicken pox, Victoria thought little of it. Chicken pox is, of course, a "completely normal" childhood virus and there was no reason to think he was in any danger. She called her pediatrician and chatted with him to be sure, then kept him home to treat him. Typical for chicken pox, especially since it's highly contagious and doctors don't want it to infect other patients in their waiting room.

It is hard to imagine anyone more qualified or capable of saving her son, but just a few days later, Chris was in the Children's Emergency Room, critically ill and fighting for his life, ravaged by a secondary strep infection. Weakened by the chicken pox, Chris' body couldn't fight the strep infection and it moved through him so quickly that by the time Victoria noticed a problem it was already too late. An asymptomatic carrier, Chris showed no signs of strep, and by the time he developed a high fever and Victoria got him to the hospital, antibiotics had no effect. Swollen with fluids, limbs blackened from a lack of circulation, and in a drug induced coma, Chris died in Victoria's arms just a few days after contracting chicken pox.

Children's hospitals serve communities all over the world. They do so with pride, professionalism, and care, sometimes facing the most heartbreaking situations. For their own sakes, hospital staff must try not to become too personally involved with a patient and family. It is quite another experience when "one of their own" checks into the hospital with a critically ill child.

"You could tell by the looks on their faces," remembers Victoria. "They knew that I knew the gravity of the situation, and it was excruciating for all of us. I asked them to tell me the truth, and they did. When Chris died, we all wept. When I returned to work several weeks later, they welcomed me back like family. They reached out to my son Ryan, my husband

and me, and provided us with a large gift basket full of tickets to Disneyland, restaurant gift certificates, and movie gift cards. They knew that the whole family would need to find a way to reunite again. I will never forget their kindness and sensitivity."

After Chris died, Victoria and Steve had a new set of challenges. "At first we were crushed and in a state of shock. How could this happen to us, to me, of all people? I am a trained medical professional—I'm supposed to know when my child needs medical care. We were vigilant parents, especially Steve, who tended to rush our children to the doctor's office at the first sign of minor symptoms. Had we hospitalized Chris sooner, would early intervention have made a difference? Would we have detected and treated the infection sooner? Would Chris have lived?"

Parents who lose children to illness, injury, or disease often blame themselves, even when it makes no sense. We convince ourselves, unfairly, that parenthood is supposed to bestow on us supernatural all-knowing, all-seeing, all-anticipating powers of perfect foresight. It makes no logical sense. How can we know the unknowable? How can we make the perfect choice 100% of the time? Just try soothing distraught parents with this logic. It's not something they can usually hear at that critical time; it's a belief they have to come to themselves. With time, most parents come back to their senses and forgive themselves, even when, to the outsider, there is nothing that needed to be forgiven in the first place. Fortunately for Victoria, she did not hold on to the guilt.

Sadly, the same was not true for Steve, who suffered self-blame long after Chris' death. Long after the doctors assured Victoria and Steve that they would have made all the same choices had it been their own child.

For the next few months, Victoria threw herself into being there for Ryan and functioning at her demanding job after she returned. "I coped with the devastation and shock by staying extremely busy. For me, that worked. I had immediate demands that had to be attended to, and these helped me keep my mind off the tragedy of losing Chris." A few weeks later when Ryan came down with chicken pox, Victoria acted immediately to test for strep and expedite antibiotics and antiviral therapy. Prepared and vigilant, Victoria made sure Ryan was never in any danger, despite his own asymptomatic strep.

Victoria wanted another child, and had been trying prior to Chris' death. Though no child could ever replace Chris, she'd always wanted three children, and now it seemed important to try again. Despite several miscarriages with in vitro fertilization in the past, she decided to try one more time with the last egg. Two months after Chris' death, Victoria was pregnant. Tragic loss and great joy juxtaposed in their lives within a month! Their beautiful daughter, Regina, was born in 1994.

Despite the pregnancy, the year after Chris' death brought real challenges for Steve and Victoria. Steve sank into a depression that he could never really shake. A couple of months after the tragedy, Steve lost his job, which made his depression worse and left him with little desire and no real need to get out of bed each day. He withdrew more and more, from the world and his family. Deeply attached to Chris, he could not or would not show up as fully for Ryan or Regina, let alone for Victoria.

Without support from Steve, Victoria looked for her own ways to cope. "When Chris died, I scoured the house to locate every picture of him. Like a woman on a mission, I framed everything and created a special photo album of Chris' short life with us. Perhaps by framing photos of Chris, I could freeze frame the time when he was still here, still with us." Unfortunately this made things worse for her husband. "What was healing for me was painful for Steve. He could not handle seeing Chris at every turn. So I took down most of the pictures, except a few of my favorites."

Her grief turned into a quest for more information about Chris' experience. "I also became obsessed with knowing Chris' whereabouts and how he was doing. As his mom, I needed first hand reassurance that he was safe and protected. Even though I am Catholic and firmly believe in an afterlife with God, I had to know that Chris was OK. I read every book I could find about near death experiences, especially those reported by children. I wanted to visit his world, to check it out for myself, and to know that he was in a good place."

Victoria believes her hopes were answered. "Chris appeared to me one night, at the foot of my bed. I was not fully asleep, nor was I fully awake. He put his hand on me, smiled and said, 'Mom, I'm OK', and then he disappeared. I have not worried about his well-being since that night."

However, this reassurance did not alleviate her anguish, and giving birth to Regina had an unexpected side effect. During midnight feedings, Victoria experienced acute grief. "I don't know why it took so long, or appeared in this delayed way, but when I fed Regina in the middle of the night, and rocked her gently, I would weep for Chris. Here was my new baby girl, who brought me such joy. Yet, I could feel Chris' presence with us at night, and I longed to hold him again too."

Victoria drew comfort from faith, family, and music. She encourages anyone who has lost a child to seek relief or spiritual nourishment in ways that speak to them. "For me it's always been the church hymns and music that bring instant comfort. When I felt most down, I would play my favorite songs in the car and they would lift me. Renee Bondi, a quadriplegic from a freak accident, had just released her first CD of spiritual songs that she created as part of her own recovery from tragedy. She has made music her ministry and it helped me heal. I was especially comforted by the song "On Eagles Wings," which we played at Chris's memorial service and is often played at my church. The music touches my soul like nothing else and I cry. My friend once told me that when she feels down or remembers tragic images, she sings one of her favorite church hymns to clear her mind of difficult images or thoughts. I've tried it, and it works!"

Victoria firmly believes in the importance of family in recovering from a crisis. While she felt more and more distant from her husband, she turned to other family members for help. "I reached out for my parents, and they were there. I have rarely seen my father cry, but he cried when Chris died. I could feel his pain, both in losing a grandson, and in watching his daughter mourn her son. We are closer today because of our shared loss. We spend more time together now and both of my parents are very close to my kids."

Victoria's marriage continued to deteriorate. Steve couldn't pull himself out of his gripping depression. While Victoria worked full-time, Steve couldn't hold down a job or bring in any meaningful income. He tried a few home-based businesses, but couldn't make them work. Devout Catholics, Victoria and Steve sought counsel from a priest, who referred them to a psychiatrist. Steve needed long-term psychiatric care to treat his chronic depression. He went through five different counselors trying to find "the right one," but never stayed with one person or course of recovery.

From Steve's point of view, Victoria never understood him or his way of grieving, yet Victoria grew weary of waiting for him to pull himself out of it. She was responsible for nearly every detail of their home life as well as maintaining her professional life. These cracks turned to full-fledged fissures when Steve's elderly father came to live with them. Soon after, Victoria lost her own job due to downsizing, a blessing in disguise as it allowed her to spend some sorely needed time with her children and revitalize her own tired, battered spirit.

Victoria prayed about their situation. Chris had been gone for four years. Steve's father died, pushing Steve further into despair and depression, yet, in Victoria's mind, he resisted moving forward or trying to heal. Finally, she asked Steve to move out, hoping a tough love approach would lead him to commit to health and resilience. When she was offered the position of Director of Pharmacy at the Children's Hospital in San Diego, she packed her children up and moved them back to her hometown, close to her parents and siblings.

Steve followed them, and Victoria hoped for the best. She continued to pray for Steve and for their marriage. They attended Retrouvaille, an intensive marriage intervention program for Catholics. Still, Steve could not connect with his children or find a way to contribute to their family, either financially or emotionally.

Six and a half years after Chris died, Victoria asked for a divorce.

Today, Victoria continues to raise her two children. She made another job change and now works at the University of California San Diego Medical Center. She met and married her new husband in 2004.

Despite her demanding schedule at work and home, Victoria was drawn into volunteering soon after Chris' death. She was asked by colleagues, who knew her story, to talk with parents who had lost children at the hospital where she had worked in Orange County. She facilitated a bereavement group at her local church. With the introduction of the chicken pox vaccine in 1995, Victoria lectured about the importance of childhood immunization to parents, pharmacists and community forums. She testified in front of a California Senate Subcommittee on Health, urging them to require the chicken pox vaccination for school entry. (The law went into effect in 2001 in California.) She has been a frequent guest speaker in national teleconferences on the subject of childhood immunization. "I guess I have a pretty compelling story to tell. Helping people get good medical care and immunizations is one way I can create some good from our loss."

Victoria made a career choice that allows her to help care for people in medical crises, though for whatever strange reason she wasn't able to help her own child in a similar situation. The aftermath of that occasion included the birth of another child, Regina, as well as the more tragic disintegration of her marriage. But Victoria grew determined to focus on healing. She reached out to family, she sought music that would uplift her, she chose to help others and she gave almost more than she had to give to keep her surviving children healthy and happy. She tried to do the same for her husband, but after six years, all of her attempts to help him heal became a burden that she could no longer bear, and she had to let him go. There's only so much one can do, for so long, to help another. At some point he has to become responsible for his own journey.

Losing a child can be a defining moment. For Victoria, it defined a lifetime of determined focus on what matters most: family, faith, and sharing your gifts and talents with others.

When asked how she has been changed by the trials of the past 12 years, Victoria quietly reflects, "If you expect God to provide for you, your way, then you're going to be disappointed. God provides, but not necessarily according to your plan. Bad things happen to good people all of the time; it's what you do with the experience that makes all of the difference."

CHAPTER TWELVE

Michelle

An open, compassionate heart. This is Michelle's gift and nemesis, offering compassion to everyone around her, and at times causing buckets of trouble in her own life. But she wouldn't have it any other way.

Born to a single mother, Michelle dreamed for as long as she can remember of a husband she could count on, and a large, loving, strong family. She married young, trained as a registered nurse, and bore five children. Sadly, her husband was not the man of her dreams. He turned out to be a philanderer. After trying for years to save her marriage, she divorced him after fifteen years and moved her family to a new county. A single mother working full-time, she relied on her older children to help raise the younger ones, a far cry from her childhood dream.

Discouraged and heavy-hearted, Michelle began her life-long spiritual quest, one that would ultimately embrace many paths and denominations, finding guidance and comfort from each without feeling the need to attach to any single one. Her discovery and exploration of Judaism, Catholicism, Protestantism, Buddhism and A Course in Miracles each offered some peace and healing, allowing her to create a unique, personal, enduring faith in the divine universe that gets her through the day, grounded and centered, aware of God's great love.

This faith and spiritual path-finding would ultimately guide her to her true calling as a compassionate, holistic caregiver for children in need. It would also help her come to terms with the fact that at times, her sympathetic nature leads her to make choices that are not easy or simple, though she knows they are the right thing to do. Part of her journey has been to accept this part of herself, and be as loving and joyful to these choices as she can be, instead of falling into regret or bitterness. This very basic choice has made all the difference in her life.

Professionally, Michelle has cared for dozens of abused and neglected children, in schools, hospitals, clinics and hospices. Personally, she has cared for more than a dozen foster-children, some critically or even terminally ill. Emotional detachment is advised in pediatrics, but Michelle has never been good at this strain of medical care, unable to turn her back on children whose needs go beyond the physical.

Michelle was profoundly changed through working with Reggie, a seventeen-year old hospice patient whose heart had been failing for six years. She came into Reggie's life only months before he died, a critical time. "I was a new nurse, with fresh eyes and no history with him. I didn't see him as 'a problem' or label him as a 'rebellious teen-ager.' I just saw him as a sweet boy who was scared to die, afraid for his mother, guilty for having been difficult, yet unable to stop acting out from fear and anger, perhaps."

"Ultimately, I took him home with me, as a foster mother.

And I think he just needed someone to tell him he was OK. I think he stayed long enough to find someone to tell him to love himself, that his mother would be alright if he left. He asked how long he could stay with me, and I told him 'forever.' It turned out to be only two short days, but I can tell you, at three o'clock in the morning, 'forever' feels overwhelming and exhausting. No matter what, though, I was determined to be there for him.

"We talked about his absent father and his emotionally distant mother, about forgiveness and being safe. During one of his wakeful periods, he attached himself to a large stuffed teddy bear that had been one of my now-grown son's, hugging it tightly. I hugged them both.

"By five a.m., after talking nearly all night, Reggie was ready for a bath, clean clothes and some oatmeal. Three hours later, he died.

"For a long time I believed that Reggie found me in order to find a safe place to die, and surely that was part of it. But I now know there's more. Reggie found me because I had lessons to learn too—lessons about time, soul connections and love, and that they are not always in direct proportion to each other. And most importantly to remember that sharing the present moment with someone who needs a companion is what counts. Reggie was buried in a snazzy three-piece white suit, with his new teddy in his arms. And I made that possible."

Michelle continued to care for children whose needs went beyond the physical. Some years later, she met Jay, a two-year-old African American in foster care after his alcoholic parents abused and neglected him. Blind in one eye, with brain shunts to reduce cerebral fluid build-up from frequent beatings, Jay exhibited constant anxiety, hyper-vigilant reflexes and a lack of trust in adults. Michelle took the bold, controversial step to adopt the little boy, despite resistance from the system and some resentment from her own five children. In the early seventies, a single Caucasian woman couldn't easily adopt an African American child. Eventually Michelle prevailed.

Michelle taught Jay to trust again, investing time, energy and patience in the emotionally scarred child, trying to make him feel loved and secure in his new world. Jay did fairly well in school and at home, and Michelle felt proud of the great strides he made.

By age 13, however, Jay began to act out by stealing, skipping school, smoking, drinking and driving Michelle's car. Michelle recognized that these teenage acts of defiance were rooted in a combination of personality, genetics and his early childhood experiences. With the help of a social worker and therapy, she learned to set clear, firm limits, and to follow through with consequences, exerting influence on the few variables she could control in Jay's life—his home life and her relationship with him. She understood, too, that Jay needed a strong father figure in his life, and she had no way to fulfill that role. Michelle did everything she could, but came to understand that for Jay to change his life, he was going to have to want to.

And he didn't.

"Watching Jay head down the wrong road was heartbreaking," she admits. "As he grew older, it became clear that his charm, physical attractiveness and people skills—strengths I thought would serve him well in adulthood—increasingly led him to making choices that seemed fun and easy in the short-run, attracting shallow, unreliable friends and an irresponsible, undisciplined attitude toward life."

Once again, a great sadness set in. Jay, her beautiful, charming, gifted son, who'd been given more than one opportunity to turn his life around, insisted on making poor choices, and having to live with the consequences. Michelle was forced to reconcile the dream of whom Jay could be, and what he might become with his talents, with the reality of who and what he chose to be. Michelle drew upon daily prayer and meditation to give her patience, strength and clarity in deciding when to intervene, and when to let go.

By thirty, Jay had fathered two children by two different women, never marrying either of them. Attracted to alcoholics and addicts suffering from low self esteem, sad products of early abuse themselves, Jay existed in a culture of chronic poverty and self-imposed limits, where earning the merit badge of "baby mama" carries status for women, even though there is scant hope of ever providing a secure, two parent home for a baby.

So the cycle perpetuates. Neither Jay nor his girlfriends were equipped or seemed concerned with providing a safe, stable, loving home for a child, at least by Michelle's standards.

When Jay's first child, a boy named Terik, was born, Michelle worked with his mom, encouraging her, teaching her mothering skills, providing money and furniture to create a good home for Terik. But after months of effort, it became painfully clear that the lure of drugs was a stronger motivation to Terik's mom than her desire to create a stable, loving environment for her son. Eventually, Michelle sued for custody to remove Terik from his unfit mother. She won. At sixty years old, Michelle became the legal guardian of a two-year old boy.

A new mixed blessing. Michelle still works full-time and then has to come home to mother a spirited, energetic toddler. She knows that simply by taking Terik out of the home he was

born into, she is offering him a life free of abuse and neglect.
Michelle allows visits from Terik's mother and her parents,
knowing that maintaining a relationship with his mother is
important to Terik, and will continue to be as he grows older.
His mother and her family believe Terik should be with them,
that the family life they offer is normal, and they resent her
interference. It's a philosophy they don't take great strides to
hide, so these visits can be challenging, emotional tightropes
that Michelle attempts to navigate with patience and grace.

Michelle's life hasn't been easy. Her choice to respond to
her heart and "what is right" has required great personal sacrifice and perhaps she has experienced more than her fair share
of disappointment. But rather than allowing life's disappoint-
ments to lead to bitterness, despair and pessimism, Michelle
has learned to reconcile the dream of what could have been,
with the daily truth of what is, releasing her expectations and
investments in a specified outcome. She does this through a
unique mix of spiritual traditions, forged by the fires of personal trial and error.

"I was raised Jewish and Catholic, so traditional ritual still
comforts me. I went to Sabbath School on Saturday morning,
Friday services when older, and Catholic Church on Sundays.
Often, I went to Rosary group on Wednesdays as well. A Rabbi
married me to a Baptist man. My children were baptized in
the Protestant Church we attended as a family. I attended the
Unitarian Church after my divorce, and began a life practice
which today also blends Buddhism with A Course in Miracles
(ACIM). Terik and I attend a family Buddhist service, and I
meditate every morning. I still find comfort in celebrating the
rituals of organized religion and I've taught Terik to enjoy them
too: Chanukah, Christmas, even Thanksgiving traditions
bring out the best in me.

"Spiritually, I try to live the principles of ACIM which means that most days I am asking for new eyes, a new way to look at a situation. I wear Buddha beads that I finger like a rosary, reminding me to stay present in the moment and to accept who or what is, just as it is.

"My advice to others is exactly the same: To realize what is, is. Take what is, and heal from that place. Don't argue with it. Of course I prefer some outcomes to others, but I have learned to accept and live with 'what is', even though some days, some events are really, really hard. It's a realization that comes with spiritual and emotional maturity. No matter how harsh the reality, you have to decide to heal. And even if you try and fail, be willing to try again and again.

"And for me, it helps that I have developed a great sense of humor. I am evolving as a human and spiritual being. I try to look for the lesson in situations, and if not the lesson, then at least the laugh!"

Michelle works as the school nurse in a special needs high school in Michigan. To the uninitiated, visiting a school for severely disabled children would be like stepping onto an alien planet, complete with its own language, gestures and culture. But it is in this alien world that Michelle's unique form of love and service has shined the brightest. Her unconventional spirituality and light-heartedness combine powerfully in a special form of ministry. "I often think that I get more resilient as I age, but that might just be that my thighs have gotten bigger and I have more bounce to my body now! I see the joy in the impaired students I work with, because I believe that I have chosen to look at them more closely. Laughter, water and music are great equalizers. I do a mean 'autistic shuffle' every year at the school prom, and I can twirl a wheelchair on the dance floor, even with my creaky knees.

"But my resilience may also be due to the simple fact that I want to be at peace, to live in a state of grace, no matter what. So I am learning how to heal, to let go, to find the joy in the moments—even when the moments may be cast against a larger backdrop of angst or conflict."

Over the past few years, Michele has taken the lessons she's learned and decided to put them to use in an even more deliberate way. She has been ordained an interfaith minister, serving quietly in the diverse communities around her. "I know the importance of just being there for someone. What I find most helpful at this stage of being a single parent/grandparent is someone willing to 'join' me in the fray, or at least be a sounding board. It doesn't happen often—there aren't a lot of working grandmothers running around looking for preschool play groups and such. I see myself as a healthy, independent woman, but I wish I had more help. Asking for help is hard for me, but necessary, and so I know the value of being there to help others, even when they don't know how to ask.

"Just being present, doing something simple—cleaning dishes, feeding a pet, shopping, and being open to accepting another in their place of need—is the most welcome gift of grace I can offer. It is hard to sit quietly and just be with someone without compulsively trying to fill the silence. This is something that I learned to do in hospice work.

"And I'm beginning to see fruit being borne from my example, another unasked-for gift. My oldest daughter, after years of resenting my 'human rescue projects,' has recently come to a new understanding of how grace works. She has offered to raise Jay's second child, Terik's step-sister, along with her own children.

"That gift is a great reminder for me, that the things I do make a difference, even when I may not see it, feel it, or even know it. Such is the nature of making a difference and maybe even changing hearts. A change of heart can happen very slowly, imperceptibly, after great resistance. So I have faith that even when the things I'm doing seem hard, the fact that I am doing them makes a difference to someone. They made a difference to Jay, and to Reggie, and to Terik, and to my daughter. Everyday they make a difference to someone, whether I know about it or not. That idea comforts me.

"Some people may look at my life and think it's been one hard, uphill struggle, or that the choices I've made make things so much harder. I understand how other people may see it that way, but I don't. I'm at peace. I feel grateful, blessed and filled with grace. I'm happy. Not just with life, in the abstract, but with *my life*—the way it is today and the path I've taken that got me here. God is good. He made me the way I am for a reason, and I've come to honor that. Looking at it that way brings me joy. Joy in Terik, joy in knowing I make a difference, joy in the journey."

Amen.

CHAPTER THIRTEEN

Karen

What, exactly, is faith? Most of us tie this word to a specific religion or system of beliefs. We take heart in knowing that our faith will bring us through, but we don't often think too intently as to the particulars. Until...

Until we lose everything. A child. Our health. A home.

Another definition of faith is trust, or confidence. And sometimes, that is enough. We believe that all will be well in the end, and Something or Someone is watching out for us, guiding us through difficult times.

In October 2003, Karen and her husband Bill were grateful to get away alone together for the first time in way too long. Only months before, they'd moved into their dream home and recently Karen had a tumor removed from her neck. She looked forward to a calm, romantic week-end without her kids, aged two and seven, whom they'd left at their suburban San Diego home with Bill's parents.

Nothing could have prepared her for the panicked phone call they received as they were preparing to come home. Karen could barely understand her terrified, crying in-laws, who said they had just evacuated because of a wildfire.

To Karen, the call made no sense. She made sure the kids were safe, and misunderstanding the urgency of the situation, asked her in-laws if they'd taken any scrapbooks or photo albums. "There wasn't time for anything," exclaimed her mother in law. "We're in the car, heading out of the neighborhood."

Karen and Bill rushed to pack, checking the news for reported wildfires in San Diego; there were none. Karen was confused. Didn't her in laws say that the entire neighborhood was evacuating? Who had authorized the evacuation? Why? Where were the emergency response teams? She couldn't dwell on these questions, and instead kept in touch with her in-laws by cell phone, making sure they were safe as she and Bill raced the 90 minutes from Orange County to San Diego to join them.

During that wild ride, Karen continually reminded herself, "The important thing is that the kids and his parents are safe. Nothing else matters." She felt immense relief and gratitude that her children were with their grandparents. She knew they'd be safe, and they'd feel more secure in the face of danger. As Karen and Bill drew closer to their hometown, they realized the magnitude of the fire, and the inability of the firefighters to control it. They had naively believed the evacuation was precautionary. What they saw confirmed otherwise. After driving into the city and witnessing raging fires, Karen will never forget how thankful she was to reunite with her children and hold them in her arms.

Karen learned later there'd been no official evacuation notice, and no report of the fire. There was also poor coordination of fire and public agencies, leaving large residential areas, like theirs, unprotected and unreported. The fires were intense and scattered, making it difficult to predict who lay in harm's way. In fact, her neighborhood had been falsely informed that the fires were miles away from them and presented no danger.

Thankfully, her neighbors had kept a close watch on the dry hills surrounding the neighborhood, standing ready with garden hoses. However, the local terrain made it difficult to see the fire until it was already bearing down on them. When giant flames crested the hill behind their neighborhood, these men and women went door to door to notify and evacuate everyone.

Alerted by these neighbors when the flames were barely 300 feet away, Karen's in-laws and her children fled the house in their pajamas. Karen's home, at the end of a cul de sac, was the first in her neighborhood to go up in flames, engulfed shortly after her family evacuated.

It took eight days to extinguish the fire that swept through their area (which came to be known as The Cedar Fire, the largest wildfire in California history). It took much longer to extinguish all the fires that ravaged Southern California. Karen and Bill waited at a friend's home, hoping and praying their home had been spared, but mentally preparing for the worst. When they were allowed back into their neighborhood, they didn't recognize it—only one single home on their street of forty-seven survived. It looked like a bombsite. Shocked and horrified, they picked through the charred remains of what had been their brand new dream home. It was a total loss. Nothing could be salvaged.

What hurt the most was losing sentimental items that could never be replaced—the baby photos, videos, first hand prints, scrapbooks; recordings of their kids' first words and the promise ring Bill gave to Karen that she'd planned to pass on to her daughter. Things could be replaced, but not ones that represented their history and memories.

In response to the disaster, Karen went into overdrive, in prayer and in action. Although she had been raised in what she calls "a mostly atheistic, neutral to anti-religious home," she prayed for strength and clarity to focus on the most important things for her family. "First things first aren't things at all; they're the people you love. When a disaster takes your home out from under you, the very foundation of your security, trust, and safety in this world is destroyed. I wanted my children to feel a sense of restored order and safety—that no matter what, we were still here, we were together, and we would keep them safe."

Within a day, Karen and Bill had rented a home close by, enabling their children to stay in the same schools. They began the process of putting their lives back together in the hundreds of small and large details that had to be handled—from shutting off services, to buying necessities and clothing, to renting furniture and filing forms for insurance. Fortunately, both Karen's and Bill's employers were incredibly supportive during this very difficult time. "I'm very grateful to them. They understood we wouldn't be able to concentrate full-time at work, while we were trying to rebuild our lives and our home. They were generous and understanding, allowing us time off to do what we needed to do."

Early on, a friend met with Karen each morning, assigning her a daily "action" list, complete with appointments, phone numbers, names, addresses and what she needed to accomplish that day. "This kind of point person is invaluable," says Karen. "When you're in the heart of a crisis, you're extremely fatigued, stressed and in a reactive mode. You are not thinking clearly. Having a good friend calmly help you focus on all of the small decisions and actions that had to take place, just for that day, made it all seem manageable. I didn't have to worry about everything all at once; I just concentrated on my daily list."

Karen's friends showed up in small and big ways to ease her family's pain and help them put their lives back together. They donated clothes and furniture. They even offered treasured photographs of Karen's children that she had given them before the fire, since she'd often acted as an unofficial photographer at community events and generously shared copies of the pictures.

Once their basic needs were met, Karen and her family looked forward to rebuilding their home and truly getting their lives back in place. But the disaster, it turned out, had not yet run its course. Before long, they learned that they, along with hundreds of homeowners facing total losses, were "underinsured." This struck Karen as patently absurd. Their home was brand new; they paid higher insurance premiums for full replacement insurance. Being "underinsured" meant that they would have insufficient insurance to rebuild the same or a similar home.

"You know how they say people facing a crisis respond with either 'fight' or 'flight'? Well, I'm all 'fight' when it comes to righting a wrong. Our homeowner's insurance policy was less than 6 months old, how could we possibly be 'underinsured?'" Karen became an activist to fight for her rights as an insured homeowner, and the rights of all of the other so-called "underinsured" owners affected by the fire. She, along with a committed team of other fire survivors ("not victims," Karen quietly asserts), took their cause to Sacramento, demanding an investigation and reform of insurance industry practices.

Investigation of the underinsurance problem revealed that many insurance carriers relied exclusively on a particular replacement cost valuation software program to value home-owner insurance policies. However, investigation showed that insurance companies and/or their agents had used a function of the software called *Quikquote* to determine replacement costs. Unfortunately that function was never designed to determine replacement cost for purposes of assigning accurate homeowners' policy limits, especially in a rapidly accelerating housing market like San Diego. Yet it was used for that very purpose, resulting in scores of homes being declared "underinsured" after the fires. Due in large part to Karen and other fire "survivors," the flaws in the software usage were uncovered and investigated. Eleven months later, the software was recalled. Legislative reform for other post-fire insurance quickly followed.

"I'm an attorney, so this was a great way to use my skill for a good cause. In retrospect, I think the 'fight' I took up on behalf of homeowners, was therapeutic. It gave me a legitimate place to channel all of my frustration, my anger, my sense of sadness for what had been lost."

Karen's family moved back into their home in July 2005 with a sense of jubilation. "Either you come through something like this feeling very blessed (for what you have), or very bitter (for what you lost). We have 'block parties' all the time now—we celebrate everything from the pouring of new sidewalks to the planting of new trees."

When asked what she's learned from this dramatic chapter in her life, Karen turns contemplative. "I am a changed person. I value my relationships even more than I did before. I am far less attached to material things. I speak my mind freely now, with much less editing. I really understand at depth the meaning and value of friends. I am stronger and wiser for the experience. Shortly before moving back to my rebuilt home in 2005, I made a big career decision, requesting (and receiving) a prized 'demotion' that would allow me to spend more time with my two young children. I loved my job, but the fire clarified my priorities."

"Besides having great friends and a Type A personality that melded well to working for a righteous cause," she muses, "prayer sustained me. I am not a religious person, but I do believe in a Power greater than myself. Prayer is the way that I was able to stay centered, calm and focused. I continue to pray on a daily basis. I pray that my family feels loved, safe and secure. I don't know how someone navigates this sort of loss without faith in something beyond themselves. Next to faith one must look to friends. Without either faith or friends, it is too much to go it alone."

Since returning to her rebuilt home in 2005, Karen has volunteered her time to United Policyholders, a nonprofit organization that educates consumers about their insurance rights. On behalf of UP, she has traveled to Louisiana and Lake Tahoe to aid victims of Hurricane Katrina and the Angora Ridge Fire.

While her own rebuilt home was spared in the 2007 Southern California wildfires, she remains actively involved in support efforts for the victims of those fires, organizing and conducting insurance information sessions.

She is also a contributing author of The Disaster Recovery Handbook and Personal Property Inventory Guide, an essential text on recovering from catastrophic property loss.

CHAPTER FOURTEEN

Judy

Here is my story, the story of losing my son Joe. I have tried to write this for three years, but each time I started to write, a deep fatigue would set in and my heart would start hurting, literally. I set out on a journey to learn from other women, to seek enlightenment from their tragic experiences and how they survived them. I'd hoped this would help me, and it did. But my heart still hurts.

I have learned to appreciate the phrase "a broken heart." My heart feels broken, more like shattered at times, shattered into a thousand pieces that represent the memories of my son, the child he was, my hopes for his future, the precious time I had with him, and how much I yearn to still be with him.

Yet with brokenness comes possibility, an invitation to heal, to become a changed person, to transcend the sadness. Do I become bitter or better? The choice is mine. And the honest answer is "Yes." To both. Some days are better than others.

I always have a choice in healing. If I am aware of my heart, I can let it crack open when it needs to. I can give it a voice and listen. I allow it to speak to me freely, to chat. I cry. I write.

I go for walks. I talk with friends. I talk to God. I chat with Joe. Today, I visit the hole in my heart, but I don't dwell in its brokenness. There is a big difference between dwelling in sadness and visiting it. Most days I choose to visit.

By definition, a broken heart is also an open heart. I offer my broken, wide-open heart to the God of my understanding, as if on an altar. I place it there with gentleness and grace. I ask God to fill the broken places with understanding, forgiveness or whatever will comfort me. I'm not an expert on healing after losing a child. I'm a beginner. I'm not particularly interested in research on the subject, though it has its place. Instead, I listen to wise mothers who have walked this path before me, with visions of ancient women gathering at village wells, drawing daily water together, for surely this must have been the original grief support group.

I don't know if what works for me will work for others. I can't heal anyone else. I can only share what has worked for me and what has worked for others. I do not own a magic wand. Well, actually I do own one—my friends gave me one recently. I wave it back and forth and say, 'Where were you when I needed you, Ms. Magic Wand?' But of course, there is no real Magic Wand that anyone can wave around and make the pain go away. Sometimes I wonder if that's what we think God or faith is—our equivalent of a spiritual magic wand? We have to somehow find a way to make our own magic, to commit to healing.

My husband Rob and I were both raised Roman Catholic, married in a Catholic Mass, and left the Church as adults to find our own faiths. In 1993, we moved to Utah, where my husband converted to the locally dominant Church of Jesus Christ of Latter Day Saints (LDS), and I settled into a Unity congregation, like I had in California. Our sons, Joe and

Tommy, attended the nearby LDS chapel with my husband, though we all honored each other's choices and often attended one church or the other as a family. We saw no inherent conflict in this; God is Love, by whatever name or path you choose.

On Sunday, January 28, 2001, I was leaving for Unity. Joe was on my computer (right here where I'm sitting now). I said to him, "Joe, I'm running late. Would you let Dad and Tommy know that I said good-bye? And Joe, I love you."

Joe, a 13-year-old who did not "transition" well, uncharacteristically spun the chair around, looked me in the eyes and said with his cherub smile, "And I love you too, Mom." (I remember feeling quite love struck by the mommy moment!)

These were the last words my son ever spoke to me. Later that day, early afternoon, a neighbor knocked on the door to tell me Joe was hurt and drove me to the church a few blocks away. I wasn't overly concerned. Joe was a fun-loving, adventurous, go-for-it boy and this was nothing new. A mild injury was the price he paid for trying out new things. I envisioned yet another trip to the Emergency Room as we'd made many times with Joe, both at home and on vacation. I once quipped to the ER admittance person, "Do you give frequent patient points here?"

I wasn't prepared for what I saw: Joe lying paralyzed on the pavement, pupils fully fixed and dilated. I knew at that moment our lives had changed forever. Crossing the street after church, he'd been hit by a car, incurring head trauma and, we'd learn later, severe brain injury. Suddenly, everything happened in slow motion, it was surreal. Paramedics arrived promptly and called for the hospital's life flight helicopter. It landed on the baseball field next to the church.

A doctor who was leaving services intubated him, enabling oxygen to flow to his damaged brain. Somewhere in the crowd, a cameraman who monitored police radio calls started filming the scene for the nightly news. A no-nonsense neighbor quickly put her hand over the camera lens, admonishing him for his insensitivity. (I will never watch TV news again without feeling outraged by the indignity of a camera zooming in on a shocked, grief-stricken family.)

The expressions of the doctor and the paramedics confirmed my fears. Joe was dying. When the helicopter arrived, I briefly argued with the crew about accompanying Joe to the hospital. Apparently, helicopter rescue protocol bars parents from flying with a critically injured child. I'm sure they have good reasons, but I was adamant. If our child died en route, either my husband or I would be there to hold him, speak his name, bless him, be with him. The flight crew understood I wouldn't budge. Not wishing to waste time, they reluctantly gave me a seat that, with a mother's prerogative, I promptly gave away to the doctor who'd saved Joe's life. I knew my son had a better chance of survival with him on board. I told him, "Do what you can to save him. And if he should die on the way, please hold him, bless him and tell him how much we loved him. I won't hold you responsible if he doesn't make it, just do your best, that's all I ask."

A friend drove my husband and me to Primary Children's Medical Center (PCMC), a 35-minute trip. We were too shocked and disoriented to drive ourselves safely. We sent Tommy, our 11-year-old son, home with friends to spare him the tumultuous emotions of the waiting room and a potentially long, difficult "death watch." Riding to the hospital, Rob took my hand and said, "Whatever happens next with Joe, we are a family, we are in this together." I felt strengthened, that somehow we would shoulder this seemingly unbearable journey together. And then a prayer came to me, one I had not consciously remembered in 30 years, the Hail Mary from my Catholic youth:

"Hail Mary, full of grace. The Lord is with thee. Blessed art thou among women, and blessed is the fruit of thy womb, Jesus. Holy Mary, Mother of God, pray for us children (my substitution for "sinners"), now and at the hour of our death, Amen."

I prayed the prayer over and over. I threw myself into it until the prayer prayed me. Then, I had a stark realization, the first of many spiritual lightening bolts to strike. If Joe was dying, I felt an urgent desire to "hand him over" to another mother, someone who would protect and love him like only a mother could. I meant no offense to God, a heavenly Father for Judeo-Christians, but I felt strongly that Joe needed, first and foremost, a mother's attention. Only a mother would understand and accept him, and provide him with the tender loving care he needed until we could be reunited in the next life. I wanted him with Mary, the quintessential, heavenly mother.

The hospital scene was crazy, bewildering. The neurosurgeon informed us bluntly, "Your son's brain is swelling quickly. He won't survive the night unless we operate to mitigate the damage."

Rob and I looked at each other and reacted reflexively. "Don't waste time talking about it, get in there and do it!" In hindsight, a million questions spring to mind I would like to have asked. What did he mean by survival? What about Joe's quality or longevity of life? And, what is the distinction between survival, keeping someone alive artificially, and restoring a meaningful life? But we didn't think of those questions. Our traumatized, instinctive response wasn't unusual or surprising—save our child at any cost!

A crowd of neighbors and friends gathered in the waiting

room, praying, giving us reassuring nods and hugs, trying to support us. I called my Unity minister and cried into the phone, "I think my son is dying. Please pray for him." He came immediately.

After surgery, the neurosurgeon told us he'd tried to mitigate the damage. He'd removed a flap of Joe's skull, allowing his swollen brain room to expand. Intracranial pressure would determine whether Joe would survive, and the next 48 hours would be critical. The brain tissue was too swollen to determine the extent of injury, but it looked catastrophic. The hospital moved Joe into the Pediatric Intensive Care Unit (PICU).

The waiting room crowd grew until the room was jammed. The grapevine had been busy and scores of friends and neighbors showed up to offer support, but we felt overwhelmed. We sat quietly with Joe in PICU, holding his hand, stroking his hair and telling him that we loved him, no matter what. I told him that Mother Mary was there for him on the other side if he needed her. If he should pass, then we would learn to accept that, and we would never stop loving him, whether he lived here or there.

We told him that he had been a delightfully fun, fearless son, and that if he could rally, we wanted him back at all costs. But we also were realistic. His chances of survival were slim. I didn't know God's will for my son; it was clear from the start that there was nothing more we, or his doctors, could do to save him. Joe was in God's hands.

Later that night, needing fresh air and a break from the frenzy, I went for a walk with a few close friends. It occurred to me to ask, "Does anyone know who hit Joe?"

Cars always drive too fast through our neighborhood, and parents continually remind their children to be careful. If I'd thought about it at all in those long, tense hours at the hospital, I suppose I'd assumed it was a stranger unfamiliar with how our "munchkins" walk all over the road, or a teenager speeding.

I knew something was wrong. They exchanged uneasy glances but didn't answer the question. So I asked again. The truth, when they finally spoke it, felt like a punch to my stomach, and my body folded in pain. The driver was a neighborhood mother. Our children had been in the same playgroup as toddlers. Worse yet, she had lost her own young daughter to a rare disease just a few years earlier.

I dialed her number as soon as I could get my hands on a cell phone. She answered on the first ring, even though it was close to midnight. She'd obviously been waiting by the phone for hours, hoping for news. "He's still alive," I said, finding myself in the odd position of comforting the driver who'd hit my son. I didn't know any of the details of the accident and it didn't matter—Joe would either survive or not. I forgave her, and I forgave Joe for whatever role he played.

Above all, I felt great sympathy for her. She knew Joe, she knew me. If she could have, I know she would have avoided hitting him, or any other child. Who among us has not had near-misses? She was a loving, kind, caring mother who had already suffered so much pain from the death of her own child.

And mentally I screamed at God, "What were you thinking? How could you place one more burden on this poor mother's shoulders? Hasn't she suffered enough already?"

These would not be the last angry words I had to say to Him.

That first night, forgiveness came easily, but I would go many rounds with that elusive virtue. As time wore on, I played the dangerous game of "if only...," a torture chamber with endless permutations. That game assumes, of course, all-knowing, absolutely predictable, superhuman qualities, which frankly we don't have—not as drivers, not as kids walking with buddies, not even as vigilant, caring parents. The "if only..." game leads to impossibly convoluted conclusions, creating a living hell on earth. With time I learned to recognize "if only...." for what it was—a flight of fantasy that assumes we could have, should have, and would have done anything to prevent Joe's accident; anything to assuage our guilt as parents; anything to bring our boy back.

Joe survived the first night, and the next, and the next. His cranial pressure measurements stabilized just below extremely dangerous levels. He lay motionless in a deep coma. Each day a team of physicians, shepherding residents-in-training, reviewed his condition. I called them the "fly by" team because their daily visits were so brief relative to the severity of Joe's condition. I came to rely on the nurses. They were the ones who explained in plain layperson's English what was happening. We bonded to our nurses like comrades in trench warfare. The extent of Joe's brain injury remained uncertain. Only time would tell.

On the fourth day Sharon, my dear friend and newly designated point person, asked, "What is your biggest wish, besides having Joe back? People want to help."

"If I can't have Joe back, then I want to know that he is never alone. And the same goes for Tommy. I want my boys to know that they are never outside our circle of love."

From that, Sharon organized a massive schedule, providing volunteer coverage for Joe from late evening to early morning. Every night at least one volunteer and sometimes two would spend the night in Joe's hospital room, enabling me to get some much-needed rest in a nearby hotel. These volunteers included our friends and neighbors, and Joe's friends from school and church. To this day I am touched by the kindness and generosity of so many people we barely knew, especially from Unity, Waterford School ,the LDS Church and our neighborhood. Some visitors read to him; some watched movies with him; others sang songs or played musical instruments. Sleepovers at the hospital with Joe continued for 90 days.

In a flash of brilliance, my husband, who owned a software development company, asked his employees to create a website so we could post updates for the growing number of "Joe fans." We received thousands of emails and other messages of support, which we read aloud to Joe. It caught fire. We asked for prayers from every nook and cranny, without regard for denomination. They came pouring in. We received notes from every corner of the country, including a Carmelite monastery in Michigan, a trailer park of retirees in Arizona, and even Mario Andretti, Joe Montana, Phil Hendrie, and several Oakland Raiders. Every single message touched us.

I've come to appreciate the power of prayer in a new light. I don't believe prayers themselves can cure someone. If that were the case, we would be rid of human suffering, illness and disease once and for all! Instead, I believe prayers engage the ones who pray in a cause beyond their own concerns. Prayers bring people, often strangers, together into a single-minded community, bonded by their mutual support of a higher cause. Prayers also remind the ones suffering that a vast circle of love and support surrounds them.

So many people were there for us, and I am grateful.

On the other hand, I grew to loathe some of the well-intentioned platitudes, like "God never gives you more than you can handle." If anyone you know is ever faced with trying circumstances, please don't say this. Personally, I wasn't particularly reassured in knowing God had so much faith in me.

Frankly, I'd rather God think me weak and useless, and have my son back.

And then, many people were praying for a miracle recovery. I felt conflicted. What was God's will, Joe's destiny? What if this accident was part of Joe's life plan? Who were we to argue? I know everyone wanted to be supportive and helpful, but sometimes I just wanted to cry, express my frustration, my panic and fear. Now I understand that the best way to support someone through tragic circumstances is to just be there with love, compassion and open arms. Don't project your beliefs or philosophies on them. Sometimes loving silence is the most powerful thing anyone can offer.

Approaching two weeks in the hospital, they turned down the ventilator, took off the neck brace, and reduced paralytic medications. Joe was able to breathe on his own, and his body was completely unharmed. He'd been lifted by the impact of the car, falling backwards, landing head-first, so his head had taken the full blow. He remained in a deep coma.

We didn't know whether to prepare for "good-bye" or "welcome back." He was going to survive, but would he recover? Would he regain any meaningful function? We were deeply anxious and troubled. Was Joe still "in there?" Was he trying desperately to return to consciousness or destined to live out his days in a vegetative state? The uncertainty exhausted us, an uncertainty that would ultimately prevail for years, not just a few weeks.

Joe's recovery would eventually require a marathon effort, with occasional sprints thrown in for good measure. And the physical, mental and spiritual exhaustion never let up. So I learned to pray for clarity, strength and courage, which felt achievable to me, rather than a miracle, which was out of our hands.

We asked to accelerate the magnetic resonance imaging (MRI) schedule in order to evaluate the extent of soft tissue damage. A team of three experienced neurosurgeons each drew different conclusions. The most senior neurosurgeon was the most pessimistic, and in the end, the most accurate, though we couldn't know it at the time.

"It doesn't look good to me," he said. "I don't like the way his brain stem looks. I don't think he is going to recover, or at least recover more than reflex functions."

The most optimistic of them disagreed, "I can't explain it, but I think he's in there. The question is: Will he find a way out? Can he rewire his neural networks to regain some functional higher cortical capability? Before we'll know, he'll need time, a long, long rehabilitation time." (Beware when a doctor repeats a word for emphasis.)

On that slim possibility, we forged ahead. We wanted to give Joe the benefit of the doubt, to believe in his rehabilitation however much the odds were stacked against him. I told him, "Joe, if you're in there and you want to try to come back, we're right here by your side all of the way through rehabilitation, however long, however hard. On the other hand, if you've had it, and you can't or don't want to come back, we're right here with you. There is nothing you can do, no injury too great or disabling that will push us away. Wherever this leads, you're our son, and we're your family. We're all in this together."

Rob and I made some important financial and division-of-labor decisions. I stayed with Joe at the hospital. Rob stayed close to home with Tommy, trying to normalize his upside-down world and fill in the much-missed companionship of his older brother. Rob, who before the accident had considered early retirement, would keep working to make as much money as humanly possible. As long as Joe was in the hospital, our health insurance covered intensive rehabilitation therapy, personal care and medical management. As with most plans, however, once he was discharged, coverage dropped to almost nothing. Severely disabled people need medication, specialized supplies, adaptive equipment, and 24/7 personal care for the rest of their lives. Rob asked me, "How much do I need to earn so we can take care of Joe for as long as he lives?" I responded, "Don't ask. It's a really, really big number, with lots of zeroes. Please, just keep working."

And so we began.

A few months into Joe's rehabilitation, there were only minor hints of recovery. I started repeating The Serenity Prayer, popular through 12-Step recovery spirituality:

God, grant me the serenity to accept the things I cannot change, (Joe's injury and recovery progress)

The courage to change the things I can, (to take care of myself and my family, to give Joe the best medical care available, to provide him comfort and companionship)

And the wisdom to know the difference. (Show me clearly what I can and cannot do; help me shed self-defeating worry about what his future holds, or anything over which I'm powerless today.)

I would begin each prayer in quiet meditation, centering myself. I didn't know if Joe would ever recover. What I did know was that we had the gift of one more day, whatever it would bring. This prayer helped me discern where to focus my time and attention, one day at a time. It was easy to fall into a reactive, exhausted, hysterical state of mind, and sometimes I did. But each morning I took the time to center myself, to ask God, "What shall I do today? How can I make a positive difference in the quality of my life and my family's life?" And I would sit in the silence, waiting for an inkling of an answer, an impulse, an idea.

Some mornings I read prayers aloud to Joe, ones left on his website, in the guest book, or from favorite prayer books, like *Illuminata,* by Marianne Williamson, *The Daily Word* or *A Course in Miracles.* I used Buddhist meditation practices to cultivate loving kindness, mindfulness, and acceptance.

Sometimes I reminded myself, "I could see peace, instead of this (a son in a coma)."

Sometimes, I wrote my own prayers.

Dear God,
You alone are the
One source of perfect love
One great physician
One who understands
One who forgives
One who holds me and shelters me from my own darkness

Please release me from fear's grip
Please release me from my dark ruminations
Please release me from my self-pitying inner child who asks,
  "Why?"
Please release me from my inner critic
Please release me from my longing for "who was, what was"
Please release me from my terror of "who he will become, what
  will be his future"
Please release me from a prison of my own design
Please quiet the questions in my heart.

Just for today, hold me in your embrace
So that I might have the strength to accept "what is"
Give me new eyes that I might see this nightmare differently

*Teach me to trust you, that "who he will become" is the same
as he has always been, loved in the beginning, now and
forever more*
Show me what to do today—in thought, word and deed,
that I might shine your light more boldly.
*Mother me that I might sleep in heavenly peace in your tender
arms*
*Father me, that I might feel safe again in your powerful
presence*
*Heal me, that the cracks of this mother's broken heart might be
mended*
Heal my family that we might find ourselves united again
Gently reel me back when I slip into crazy reactive thinking
Love me every step of the way, no matter where this leads
*Guide me in doing the same for my family and others close to
Joe*
*Speak to those who follow this unfolding story of their own
lessons in love*
*That they might discover insight, strength and courage to heal
their own lives*
Remind me that Joe was first your son, before he was ours
*And that we all want the same thing for him—love, peace,
acceptance, and oneness*

You alone can heal Joe, you alone can heal us
And you alone will
If we let you.

Thank you God, Amen.

I wanted to hold a believing space for Joe's recovery, and
at the same time, I wanted him to know that he was loved "as
is," that he didn't have to improve for us to love him any more

than we did. This insight came to me when I watched moms of children born severely disabled. They loved their children "as is"; they'd never known their children any other way. I wondered how it was for Joe, to be stared at, people wishing he'd get better, reminding him of who he used to be and longing for that person's return. Is it the same for older patients with Alzheimer's or dementia? Who among us would welcome that sort of companionship? You used to be somebody—please come back the way you were.

Days slipped into weeks, weeks into months. I became friends with PCMC's chaplain, Michael. When he'd ask me how I was holding up, I'd tell him I was getting by, a day at a time...some better than others. One day, candidly I said, "You know, the thing that drives me crazy is the miracle story. You know, the type... when the man sits up after spending six months in a coma and is completely cured, perfect in every way. We don't even know yet if there's *any* recovery in Joe's future, let alone a *miracle recovery*. The way Joe is today may be as good as it gets. Why can't people see this, that their miracle stories are hurtful, not helpful?"

Michael smiled in his gentle way, "Do you know why they tell miracle stories?"

"No," I shook my head, "I guess they want to give us hope?"

Michael nodded, "Well, that's part of it....But I think they tell a miracle story because they need to hear it."

"Why? They know how it comes out in the end!" I challenged.

"They need to hear it again because they need to feel reassured. They don't know how to be with you in your pain and uncertainty; it's too much for them to bear. So they tell themselves a story with a happy ending *that brings them* the comfort, hope and certainty that they crave, for themselves and for you. They don't know any other way to support you, other than to hope and pray for a happy ending....it's the only way they can feel OK about where Joe is right now."

I was astonished. Another spiritual lightening bolt! "Oh, I get it. *I will listen to comfort and support them in their need to feel OK about Joe!* This is a great insight! From now on, I won't take these stories so personally."

On a poster in Joe's room where visitors could write notes, someone had written, "Joe, we are praying for a miracle for you." Next to the quote I wrote, *"Joe, you are the miracle."*

Joe's room overlooked the main entrance to the hospital, where I had a bird's eye view of departures. Grateful families embraced their children like returning war heroes. Balloons, flowers and stuffed animals marked these joyful celebrations. It was an amazing, gratifying spectacle—so many children able to walk, wheel their way out of the hospital, hugged by nurses and doctors, ready to re-enter the world, whole and healed.

I dubbed Joe's room "the womb with a view." I fantasized that one day we would be among those happy, healthy families.

But that was not to be. The hospital gave their best effort, but after three months Joe was released due to lack of progress. His discharge was heartbreaking. There were no balloons, no flowers, no well-wishers. Instead, a medical transport van pulled up and I wheeled him in, to be taken to another rehabilitation hospital, known as a "step down" facility.

Aptly named, considering how well it describes one's diminished dreams.

Despite my daily acceptance ritual, anger had been simmering for some time. Someone had to be held accountable for what had happened to Joe, or so I thought, and it was time to wrestle with God, the capricious, arbitrary Being of my then-limited understanding.

"Why do you cure some children, and not others?" I railed at Him as Joe and I made the journey to "stepping down." "Are they not all your children, loved equally? Were some children more deserving or better prayed for? How are we supposed to accept the claim of Your all-loving, all-knowing protection when some of our children leave this hospital sick, diseased or disabled? And what about the dead children who are quietly removed through the back elevators and hallways? Were they less deserving of a miracle than the children in the hospital beds next to them? If there's a lesson in all of this, no loving teacher would use a child's death to make a point!" I figured if I had a true intimacy with God, then He could take the brunt of my honest lamentation and not abandon me.

Another spiritual lightening bolt.

My historical notion of an all-knowing, all-powerful God was under siege, and I was doing the attacking. I returned to praying to Mother Mary. She, of all people, the ultimate Jewish mother, hand-picked to bear the son of God, Jesus. She would understand.

Through whatever religious lens one views the crucifixion story, I try to imagine what that must have been like for Mary, watching helplessly as her son suffered excruciating torment and pain.

As we settled Joe into his new hospital, a thought entered my mind, took root and grew. Joe might not recover, no matter what we did, no matter how hard he or we tried. God could cure Joe, if He chose to, but He might not.

If that was true, then how might I find peace with who Joe is now, rather than wish for the Joe who used to be? Refrains from the psalms repeated in my head as I drove to the hospital each morning:

"I will love you with an everlasting love."

"As a mother comforts her child, so too will I comfort you."
    I begrudgingly accepted God, the original source of Love, as my constant companion, but I demoted Him from CEO. Gone was the directing, controlling and intervening God. I couldn't believe in Him. I replaced that God with One who would companion me and hold my hand, to hell and back if needed.

I didn't care much for theological dogma or religious concepts anymore, especially those espoused by others who "got their miracles." I had to find a way to be with Joe—and the whole situation—that would not leave me hopeless, helpless and in utter despair. I had to support my family in finding a "new normal" that included some measure of happiness again.

Now settled into HealthSouth Rehabilitation Hospital, Joe continued to receive daily therapy, quality care and medical supervision by an excellent neurologist. For 13 long months we tried everything that modern western medicine could offer: trial medications, aggressive physical, occupational and speech therapies, electrical stimulation and adaptive devices. We also tried everything that alternative medicine could offer: watsu, acupuncture, cranial sacral, reiki, massage, music and pet therapy. And we continued to pray.

Despite our best efforts, Joe's progress was limited. Although no longer in a coma, he remained in a vegetative state. He could not speak, eat food by mouth, control his bladder or bowels, or move his body volitionally.

Even in this limited state, Joe attended Jordan Valley School, a special needs public school less than a mile from the hospital. There, a spirited, caring staff, who were used to kids like Joe, tirelessly tried to help him: They used software to stimulate his neural networks, augmentative communication devices, walkers, standers, water therapy, snoezelen stimulation and (Joe's favorite) friendly daily banter designed to provoke a response. Joe even competed in the teachers' weekly NFL betting pool. Joe "picked" his winning teams by winking, nodding or twitching—the meaning was left up to the interpretation of his teachers. Much to everyone's surprise, one week he beat 28 teachers and won the pool!

Five months after the accident, Joe finally responded to stimulation. He grinned and laughed out loud, a deep chortle, while Rob told him the story of their first father-son wrestling match, which Joe won due to "dirty tactics." We were stunned. Joe laughed aloud in response to the story! At the time, we considered it a break-through, what we hoped would be the first of many steps in Joe's emerging responsiveness.

In fact, his ability to laugh was the only meaningful function he would ever recover. He smiled, he chuckled, and he guffawed at things that struck him as funny. He especially enjoyed potty humor and teenage off-color jokes. It became a challenge to make Joe laugh, one that his medical staff and teachers readily accepted. Adding to the challenge was Joe's unpredictability. Sometimes he laughed aloud; sometimes he just looked past you with glazed eyes.

It was a bizarre mystery. I asked the neurologist how someone in a vegetative state could respond to humor. He couldn't explain it. For the most part, Joe's other reactions were reflexive. So, we didn't understand it, but we came to accept him as "our new Joe," restoring one of the essential life skills that we all require in the darkest of times—humor.

Sixteen months after the accident, the hospital discharged Joe and we brought him home. A bittersweet moment; it reminded me of his first homecoming as a newborn. Joe was coming home with many of the same needs—to be dressed, fed, diapered, bathed, lifted. But as a newborn, the future stretched out in front of us, full of excitement and possibility. This time, it seemed so tragic. He was 14 years old, 6 feet tall and 175 pounds. He had no future, as far as we could tell.

I harbored a quiet hope that bringing him home, surrounding him with his family, pets, with familiar sounds and smells would bring progress, but it was not to be.

He seemed happier, more relaxed at home. He enjoyed hearing Rob's teasing voice, feeling my tender touch. He loved being with Tommy again. My sense is he knew he was home, and this gave us some sense of togetherness again in spite of the enormous demands of his ongoing care and learning to adjust to "our new Joe."

I hired student nurses to help me part-time, fearing I'd become overwhelmed, depressed and fatigued if I tried to take care of Joe on my own. I asked a young couple to move in with us, to help me with Joe's therapy, in exchange for housing. I knew that self-care was essential, and hiring help gave me the time I needed to recharge and to spend quality time with family and friends. I was so grateful to Rob and his employer, that we had the resources to hire qualified help. I know so many home caregivers don't have that luxury.

Even with help, it was difficult. I attended conferences devoted to brain injury and caring for the severely disabled, where they warned of "caregiver morbidity," a term that sounds as bad as it is. Joe was totally disabled; I was not. I promised myself that I would not live an unlived life, in a slow death march to the grave. I loved Joe, *but* I would not let perpetual suffering become the measure of my devotion.

As part of my own ongoing recovery during the years I was Joe's primary caregiver, I burrowed deeply into the world's religions to see what they could teach me. In desperate need of something beyond full time care giving, I enrolled in an interfaith seminary program in New York City, One Spirit Interfaith Seminary, where I could do distance studies. Asked why I was enrolling, I answered honestly, "I need something to hang on to right now, something other than the relentless demands of care-giving, and mourning the loss of my son."

"Oh, I'm so sorry, did your son die recently?"

I hesitated. How complicated trying to describe what it was like with Joe. "No, there are some things worse than death. My son is still here physically, but because of a severe brain injury, 'he' is not here anymore, someone else is here instead." I went on to explain that I needed a spiritual life raft to cling to, to keep me afloat, until I could learn how to endure this ordeal with grace. I don't think I fit the profile of what they were seeking in ministerial candidates, but they took pity on me and accepted me into the 2-year program.

We presume those drawn to ministry are called to serve others, but it wasn't like that for me. I was merely trying to survive. Joe's nonstop care, his lack of recovery and worry for his and our family's future, sapped me of every ounce of energy. Practicing extreme self-care became essential, and to me, exploring the world of spiritual possibility became part of that care. It may sound selfish, to think about one's own health, state of mind and spiritual nourishment first, but in fact, nothing could be further from the truth. As part of seminary training, the director reminded us, "You cannot serve from an empty well. Fill your well first that you might serve others."

I took her words to heart. I filled my well—physically, emotionally, mentally and spiritually. I acted as if I had suffered a severe injury, as if I were in acute rehabilitation for invisible wounds to the heart and soul. For physical renewal, I ate nutritious foods, I slept long hours (once I figured out how to get Joe to sleep a full night), and I exercised daily, taking in fresh air and sunlight whenever possible.

To nourish myself mentally, I studied the world's great religions and completed my homework in an attempt to jumpstart my own damaged cognitive abilities. Emotionally, I scheduled time for me, and with my family—for dinners, walks with my husband, comedic movies at home, Tommy's sports and school events. I also joined fun, caring friends for hiking, skiing or lunch.

Spiritually, I worked intensively with time honored practices—mantras, body prayers, meditation, *lectio divina,* chanting, singing, recitation of prayer, psalms and scripture. I attended different worship services when I could. I tried to imagine how the world's great religious teachers through the ages might counsel me in my predicament.

I was determined to survive, as healthy and whole as possible. Changed, of course. A different person. But a whole one, even if the shattered pieces looked glued back together at the seams.

I became equally determined that Tommy would not be robbed of his precious childhood years. At some point in the future, many years after Joe's accident, if he was asked the question, "What was your childhood like?" I wanted him to be able to answer, "I had a great childhood. Yes, I lost my big brother in an accident, and that was hard, we were very close. But I had good parents who really loved me and they gave me a wonderful childhood!"

We're a family. That means every one counts, not just the injured one. In the two years that Joe lived at home after his accident, we attended every one of Tommy's athletic and school events, and we went on vacations to Hawaii and Orlando. Whenever possible, Rob came home early from work to spend time with Tommy, taking him to bowl, play golf, play "skill crane" or just to goof off.

Joe's accident happened on January 28, which was Super Bowl Sunday. It's impossible to erase the sadness swirling around the "accident anniversary," but Rob created a new tradition to reverse the emotional tide of that day. Since the accident, he has taken Tommy to the Super Bowl every year, no matter where it's played.

One of the most painful aspects of the accident is that, while we lost our son, Tommy lost his only brother, leaving a huge void in his life. The brothers had been best friends and constant playmates all of their lives. Overnight, the "boys' noise" disappeared; our home became eerily quiet. We went to great lengths to include Tommy's friends in sleepovers and outings, and to encourage them to include Tommy in theirs.

By spring 2004, three years after the accident, Joe developed seizures and pneumonia. We knew in our hearts it was the beginning of the end. Our "long good-bye" with Joe would soon be over. As I felt Joe slipping away, I started attending daily Catholic Mass at a nearby parish. Returning to the traditional ritual of my early Catholic education was instinctive, like a salmon returning to its spawning grounds.

I listened, I knelt in prayer, I lit candles, I recited the familiar refrains, and I took communion. I didn't worry whether I was a member of the parish or even an "active Catholic" worthy of this sacrament. I just crawled in on my knees— humbled, exhausted and terrified.

What if heaven is just a sweet fairy tale designed to make us feel better about dying? Where is my son going? What will he do there? Who will be with him? Who will remind him that he is loved?

The priest sensed my anguish, though we never spoke of

it. I told him I was "deeply troubled" and looking for spiritual support. After Mass, I would sit in front of a statue of the Mother Mary in the garden, where she stood half-smiling with open arms. And I would cry and ask her for help. I asked her to be by my side, by my family's side, as we walked this last, most difficult leg of the journey with Joe. Only she would understand what we were facing.

I also prepared to hand Joe over to his deceased ancestors, in the Native American tradition, so he would be "recognized and welcomed" in his new life. At home, on my bed stand, I encircled Joe's baby picture with photos of Grandmother Bickel and Grandfather Wolf. I asked them to be there to greet Joe, to reassure him that he had a loving family in the next life too. Once upon a time, naïve and carefree, I'd assumed I'd be there for Joe as he crossed that threshold. Now I urgently called in proxies.

We moved Joe into Care Source hospice for privacy and access to palliative care. He only lived there four days, but they were serene, peaceful days. On April 13, 2004, Joe drew his last breath, surrounded by a prayer circle of my friends, with Rob and Tommy nearby. We didn't expect him to die at that moment, though his health was failing. We were preparing to say good-bye in a loving, prayerful way, but based on the hospice doctor's estimate, we expected to have him for three or four more days.

I whispered in Joe's ear that it was OK to let go, to say good-bye; he had been a wonderful son, and it was time to go home to God. My friend Lori led a beautiful guided meditation, describing a lavish banquet table surrounded by excited family and friends, all waiting for Joe's arrival. In the meditation, Jesus pulled the guest of honor chair out and summoned Joe to sit next to Mother Mary, and right at that moment, as if on cue, Joe left this world, with no struggle. He just drew a quiet, final breath and let go.

We were shocked. None of us expected it to happen; none of us had ever witnessed a death. It took me a moment to realize Joe wasn't in his body any more, that he had gone home. I called Rob and Tommy into Joe's room and we said our final good-byes to a beloved son and brother, and, respecting his sense of humor to the last, asked him to please stay out of trouble on the other side.

Saying good-bye was difficult, but we had no regrets. We had given Joe a great life, the best that we could. We'd left no words unsaid, the true gift of a long good-bye. It was important to me to honor and dignify his final passage, to make it a sacred time, on par with his arrival on earth. I handed Joe over to Mary his mother, to Jesus his brother, and to his deceased grandparents. A teacher of Joe's once described him as a "loveable pain in the ass." I'm sure all hell broke loose as soon as he stepped over to the other side—and they called for reinforcements as soon as possible!

A few days later later, we held a memorial service in our neighborhood LDS chapel, the one Joe had attended before the accident. My friend Sharon gave the eulogy. She had known Joe since he was born and expressed so beautifully some of the lessons from the last chapter of his life. I offer some of her words here:

"I don't know why the accident happened, but I know that it brought about miracles. Joe's accident healed some part of everyone who came in contact with him, even those who had never met him before. Joe, even in his very limited state, had a way of endearing himself to people. It was hard to explain. He illuminated love in unexpected and startling ways. There was

something about Joe's story that reached deeply inside us—
that wrenched our hearts open. It was as if in the forced still-
ness of his life, his enormous courage and heart shone through.
People simply answered an inner call to serve and showed up
for Joe."

I listened to Sharon's words with a deep sense of gratitude. When I stood at the pulpit and looked out at the large
assembly of people, I had a distinct sense of what it truly meant
to "love one another." Each person attending Joe's memorial
had helped, and some had been there every step of the way.

I could see the different pockets of people who had touched
Joe and us—our families, LDS, Unity, Waterford, Jordan Valley, his sports teams, neighbors, my prayer circle, my hiking
and ski groups, PCMC and Health South, other parents of
severely disabled children and our beloved student nurses and
therapists.

Looking out at the audience, I understood how we tem-
porarily bond together as one people, one family, when something bigger rallies us to a higher purpose. I had a new understanding of "family," that we can choose how widely we will
draw our family's circle of love. And like a large (at times dys-
functional) family, we will continue to squabble over differences in spiritual beliefs and practices. Sometimes we will even
kill over those differences, when we let hatred take root. There
is something about us human beings—we love to be right, to
know what the future holds, to feel safe and secure. But nothing could be further from the reality of what it is to be a human being. Life by its very nature is a risky proposition. Only
death is certain, and it may not be timely or convenient, or
even kind enough to give us advance notice.

What does it mean to "love one another?" It means to show
up and be there for someone in need, no matter what the prog-

nosis or the outcome. Why? Because we're all in this life to-gether. Nobody's getting out of this alive. Joe, in his totally disabled state succeeded in doing what few others with full faculties could do—bring hundreds of people together for a higher purpose to a place where denominational differences did not matter. "Love one another" to me means to walk gen-tly next to your brothers and sisters, offering them compas-sion—to companion them in their passion.

As a final gift of life Joe's organs and tissues were donated. We later learned that a baby boy in California received Joe's corneas. How perfect! The twinkle in Joe's beautiful mischie-vous eyes lives on in this world!

As I reflect on these lessons now, three years after Joe's death, I realize they are part of my inner spiritual life, part of my relationships, part of my practice as an interfaith minister. The sadness of losing my son never goes away. It quietly re-cedes into the background like a wave pulling back and gath-ering power. And like a rogue wave, it can suddenly bring me to my knees with its crushing pain, often when I least expect it. Then, by the grace of God, I find a way to crawl back, struggle to regain my footing and take another shaky step forward. Often God's grace shows up in a friend who picks me up when I can no longer do it for myself. I trust that God and I will continue to walk every step of this painful, mysterious and wonderful journey together, no matter where it leads. My re-ligion today is acceptance.

7 Lessons Learned and a Leaping Off Point for Further Discussion

In writing this book, I sought sage counsel from women who had come before me, following in their footsteps toward hope and healing. I traveled to that ancient village well, seeking comfort, help, wisdom and understanding, determined to learn how to heal, for myself, and for fellow travelers. Grief literature is replete with wonderful suggestions for emotional healing, but pretty silent about the spiritual kind (except to say it's important that you follow your own beliefs.) Regardless of faith or spiritual orientation, each woman in this book has a powerful truth to share, if you're willing to consider her message with an open mind and heart. However, I noticed that certain important themes resurfaced again and again and I've come to understand their value in the process.

1. Healing is a choice. It may sound harsh, cold, and unsympathetic. No one can force you to heal. It's in your court. It's a decision, a commitment. These women were activists in their own healing journey. At first consumed by their pain, and mired in numbness, shock, and disbelief, they felt great sorrow, but chose to re-engage in life. They made a choice to affirm life over death, even when they didn't necessarily "feel like it." At some point, if you want to feel alive again, you may need to practice "tough self-love," forcing yourself to move forward. Take care of yourself, even when it feels selfish or doesn't lessen the pain. Love yourself. Treat yourself like you would a best friend, with tenderness, compassion and patience. You're doing the best that you can under the circumstances! Just keep moving as if your life depended on it, because it does.

2. Healing is unique, like your fingerprint. Find your own way. Pick a recognized spiritual path or blaze your own trail. But walk it, one day at a time. If the spiritual path you're on isn't working for you, perhaps you need to give yourself permission to explore other options. If not another religion, then maybe another church. Or a journal, unedited letters to God. Or a simple mantra, "God, please show me the way to peace." Authentic spiritual paths are all valid; they are all valuable. But they are only truly effective if they help you connect to Spirit when you need them most, and you *actually use them.* The women in this book moved toward a God (by whatever name) of love, mercy and compassion, a God who they could trust to heal their brokenness. No matter what the religion, they shared common practices we can all find comfort in: meditation, scripture study, therapy, support groups, nature, ritual and connecting deeply with a like-minded community.

3. Healing takes time, and is hard work. After months of intense effort in acute rehabilitation with Joe, I envisioned a similar metaphor for me. I was in acute rehabilitation for my broken heart, my wounded spirit. It was time to invest in my recovery, to restore my sense of being alive. Review the women's stories that inspired you most. What did they do to affirm life, to re-engage? Put together your own personalized "get well" program, and work it with rigor, especially when you don't feel like it. Ask for help. Recruit a personal coach to encourage you—a friend, therapist, clergy or support group. Don't concern yourself with others' expectations or timelines for your healing. You know yourself best; just keep moving forward in your own way, your own pace. Stay with it.

4. Healing is messy. Your heart is shattered, your soul deeply wounded. You'll likely feel "crazy" at times—physically exhausted, emotionally overwhelmed, mentally impaired, spiritually adrift. Be gentle with yourself. These are all normal, natural reactions. Allow yourself to release these intense emotions in non-destructive ways. I like to call it, "vomit it out," a crude but apt description. Find ways to "vomit out the pain"— sobbing, throwing tantrums or objects (safely please!), wailing, crying while walking in nature, journaling, talking to your deceased loved one, writing them letters, etc. The women in these stories employed a range of "vomit it out" techniques. They did not deny, repress, or deaden themselves to their pain. Their journey was wild and unpredictable. There were peaks and valleys, and surprise setbacks. Expect the unexpected. Start each day in a centering spiritual practice—quieting the mind, opening the heart, asking for direction, strength, comfort from your Source. End each day the same way, with whatever spiritual practice works best for you. Open and close each day—it's done. Don't ask, "How long will it take until I feel happy again?" It will come slowly, like the first light of dawn, and then it will disappear again in a fog, only to reappear when you least expect it. Healing is achieved one day, one moment at a time.

5. Healing is holistic. Our brokenness manifests in physical, mental, emotional and spiritual pain. There are no clear boundaries—where does emotional healing end and spiritual healing begin? Practicing good self-care in the physical realm —healthy diet, exercise and sleep—promotes emotional and mental healing. Daily spiritual practice—prayer, meditation, yoga, walks with God, scripture study, chanting, rituals or whatever attunes you to God's love—promotes clarity of mind and calmness of heart. They are all interdependent. Use all of these dimensions to support your healing. Make your healing a priority. Before taking on a new demand on your time or energy, ask yourself, "Will this activity help or hurt my healing? My family's healing?" Be rigorous about protecting your time and commitment to healing.

6. Healing requires community. We cannot heal in isolation, although some of the hard work is done in solitude. Each of these women found their own version of a support group, community or coach to keep them moving forward in the process. Secular support groups are widely available in major cities, online and through hospitals and nonprofits. Your personal coach might be a therapist, a clergy member, a friend or family member, or a compassionate soul who has walked the path before you. This may be one of the biggest advantages of regular participation in a church or spiritual community, natural gathering places for like-minded people. We can't anticipate life's tragedies, but all faiths deal with human suffering, offering a theological, spiritual framework for coping, as well as a human network of support. Even if you're a broken stranger crawling in on your knees, a healthy church will embrace you "as is" and help you with the best tools they have. Often people return to their church of origin in times of great suffering, even if they've been absent for years. Familiarity is comforting. Don't overlook this route, even if (especially if?) you're mad at God, the universe or whomever you blame for your loss. If you don't have a church, look for a new church or spiritual community.....God, in all of His clever disguises, will be there too. Go to where Love is, where you resonate with the presence of love as manifested there. Think of it as a safe port in a heavy storm; don't worry about whether you agree 100% with the theology or like all of the members. Try out different churches or spiritual practice communities, until you find one that feels right for you. Participate regularly to fuel your momentum.

7. Healing is promoted by gratitude and service. You haven't lost every one you've ever loved; you've lost one or a few. You haven't lost all of your physical functioning; you're just more limited now. You haven't lost every thing that matters to you; you've lost your home, not your family. Gratitude is a cornerstone of all spiritual traditions. Why? Quite simply, it works. You will feel better if you practice gratitude, even though at first it may be a stretch. What we focus on grows. Conscious gratitude takes different forms—some women journal 5 things every day for which they're grateful, others express gratitude in the form of a prayer, a letter or a helping hand to someone else. Reaching out to help someone is one of the best ways to stoke the fires of gratitude and reconciliation. It's not so important that you "feel" grateful, it's more important that you express and demonstrate gratitude. Often it's the action that kick-starts the emotion. Some people take on causes or donate time and resources to honor their deceased loved ones, or to help others with a similar health problem, loss or tragedy. If you're ready to expend the energy, this can be a fruitful way to "vomit out" your personal pain through affirmative action. Just remember to move at your own pace; don't let others push you into action before you're ready. Don't let others, especially those who have not walked in your shoes, tell you anything about what you "should" be doing, period. Adopt a gratitude practice, work it, and ask the God of your understanding to guide you to the right person, right time, right situation where you can serve another person in need. All of these women engaged in meaningful acts of service, some more quickly than others. Some took on large causes, some reached out to a single person, one at a time. It's not the form or magnitude of service that matters. It's that your heart is engaged in helping someone else, in a way that you find meaningful. And slowly, you feel a little better each time you give a heartfelt piece of yourself away.

Each of these women has influenced my own healing, in ways that I cannot even comprehend, much less express. I am especially grateful for their patience, courage, generosity and trust—to bare their thoughts, hearts and souls to me, and through me, that we might all be served.

Thanks, my dear friends, teachers and sisters at the well. Today, I reach out and take the hand of the newest newcomer. I will draw her close, offer her a drink poured from these blessed waters, and I will teach her what you have taught me by your powerful example. Thank you, and May the God of all sacred names, and none, bless you on your journey.

"True religion is real living; living with all one's soul, with all one's goodness, all one's honesty."
– Albert Einstein

Judy with her family.

About the Author

Judy Wolf is a wife of 27 years, a mother of two wonderful sons, and an interfaith minister who describes her contribution as "ministry by wandering around" or "faith without borders," serving in the cracks and crevices between denominations. Based in Salt Lake City, she serves people who are hurting, regardless of their faith affiliation, religious beliefs or spiritual orientation. She is called into sensitive hospital or hospice situations, especially those involving children, and uses her own painful experience to help families navigate difficult situations. Known for her candid, direct and humorous style, she is a regular guest speaker at regional health care conferences. She also conducts weddings, funerals, baby blessings and other sacred ceremonies where multiple faiths are represented or there is no faith affiliation. Judy earned a B.A. in Economics and Political Science from UC Berkeley, an MBA from St. Mary's College of California, and was ordained an Interfaith Minister by One Spirit Interfaith Seminary in New York City. In her prior professional life, she was a human resources manager, specializing in training and development.

Spiritual Life Rafts is her first book.